David Leadbetter's
POSITIVE
PRACTICE

David Leadbetter's
POSITIVE PRACTICE

David Leadbetter

with Richard Simmons

Photography
DAVE CANNON

Illustrations
DAVE F. SMITH

HarperResource
An Imprint of HarperCollinsPublishers
www.harpercollins.com

Dedication:
For Kelly, Andy, Hally and James

For information, address HarperCollinsPublishers, Inc.
10 East 53rd Street, New York, NY 10022

HarperCollins books may be purchased for educational,
business or sales promotional use. For information, please write:
Special Markets Department, HarperCollinsPublishers, Inc.,
10 East 53rd Street, New York, NY 10022

Flexibility exercises courtesy of Chris Verna
Strength exercises courtesy of Pat Etcheberry

Additional photography:
Simon Bruty/Allsport p 8
Jonathan Daniel/Allsport p 12
Stephen Munday/Allsport pp 6/7, 14, 136

Designed and produced by
Cooling Brown, Middlesex, England

Color reproduction by
United Graphic Pte Ltd, Singapore

LIBRARY OF CONGRESS CATALOGING-IN-PUBLICATION DATA
AVAILABLE UPON REQUEST

ISBN 0-06-272070-8

05 06 07 08 ◆ 10 9 8 7 6 5 4 3 2 1

Printed and bound in China

CONTENTS

If you want to reach your true potential as a golfer, find a competent teaching professional who will help map out the direction your game should follow. Be aware of your destination and understand the route to your goals. Enjoy the journey, and try to have fun on the way.

INTRODUCTION

I SPEND MOST OF my working days out on the practice range. Hardly a glamorous 'office', but I would choose it over a fancy view in a high-rise glass-walled block any day. There's really no better place for someone so intrigued with the nuts and bolts of the swing and the complexities of the learning process to while away the hours, and I get a great deal of satisfaction when I see a student improve – whether that's a beginner just about getting the ball into the air, or a tour player fine-tuning his or her method to shape a certain shot. Which explains my enthusiasm for this particular book – observations on learning golf, dedicated to the art of *practicing* golf.

More and more people around the world are discovering the mystery and fascination of this wonderful game, and yet, at the general 'club' level, the standard hasn't improved much in recent years. It gives me no great pleasure to suggest that the average player is someone who shoots around the mid-90's, who, on a good day, might hit just two or three greens in regulation, has an acute sand phobia, and struggles to take fewer than 36 putts in a round. But, sadly, it's all too true.

These figures surprise some people, but they don't surprise me. I've seen too much hard evidence. Take a look around your own club this weekend. You'll see golfers turn out to play in such a hurry they don't even have a few minutes to loosen up their golfing muscles or stroke a few putts before they tee-off. So they make a hash of the first few holes, throw away shots faster than you can count them, and then wonder why it is their game only begins to click on the back nine.

Those who do make it to the range are not always better off. Too many players think a balanced warm-up session involves flirting briefly with the mid and short irons before wrapping their hands around the driver and hammering balls toward the far boundary fence. By the time they've finished, their tempo is shot for the day.

THINKING YOUR WAY TO A BETTER GAME...
Good golf is *smart* golf, both on and off the course. It's certainly no coincidence that the players who continue to be successful are good thinkers when it comes down to analyzing performance and working on specific facets of their game out on the practice area. And there's the rub. Whatever your dreams and ambitions in this game may be, unless you are prepared to invest a certain amount of time and effort to improve your skills through formulated practice, golf will continue to get the better of you.

◁ *In Japan, where golf courses are inaccessible and prohibitively expensive, practice is regarded as a 'sport within a sport', and multi-level ranges like this one in Tokyo are commonplace. The majority of golfers here set foot on a real course perhaps once or twice a year – if they're lucky.*

A reasoned approach to practice involves little more than common sense. The first thing I do with a new pupil is run through his or her recent form. I talk to the player about specific aspects of the game and, once out on the range, make mental notes on the general standard of their ball-striking, any problem shots they might be experiencing, the quality of their short-game skills relative to the rest of the game, and so on. Not only does this exercise help me to get to the root of the problems that most need attention, it provides the players I coach with a clear perspective on their game, and so enables them to set their sights on *realistic* practice targets, which is always important.

Such a 'pencil-and-paper' examination of your own game is vital if you are to make good use of this book, so before you next go out to play, set aside some time to study the opening chapter, which deals specifically with this process of self-analysis. Noting and regularly updating your performance figures opens the door to immediate improvement, for as a pattern emerges so will a list of 'priorities' in terms of the time you should devote to working on certain skills. Rather than beating balls and making the same old mistakes, you can instead begin to *practice with a purpose*.

Whether you are a single-figure player shooting in the low 70's, or a long-handicapper desperate to break through the 100 barrier, the short-game figures are most likely to grab your attention: i.e. your pitching, chipping, sand-save and putting stats. Even the briefest of calculations will reveal that over half the shots you play in 18 holes are from within 100 yards of the flag. So it makes sense that at least half your practice time should be devoted to sharpening these short-game skills. Probably more.

Nothing is more important than turning three (or four!) shots into two. Feeling comfortable with the slightest swing change takes time, patience and practice. Generally improving the quality of your ball-striking can take a while, too. But trimming a few shots off your score with some dedicated short-game work is something every single golfer can achieve, almost immediately.

"*It's alright for the pro who plays and practices every day, I just don't have the time…*" This is a statement I hear all too often, and time is a significant factor, no doubt about it. But there are ways and means of maximizing the productivity of whatever time you can spare. Toward the back of the book you will find listed a number of suggested practice schedules which take into account a limited time-frame. Once you have identified your weaknesses you can use the drills littered throughout the book to improve specific facets of your game, and plan a schedule around whatever time you do have available. Set your own agenda. Some golfers

▷ *The young Swedish players I teach are particularly motivated to learn and improve, focused on becoming the best they can be. Avid practicers, they grew up in a culture which places great emphasis on self-improvement – witness the Dome, a state-of-the-art practice facility in Stockholm.*

love to practice, others just want to play. But somewhere in here there's a balance that will satisfy you as an individual.

If you have access to good facilities – i.e. a good hitting surface, with specific targets to aim at, yardage markers to indicate distances, and a well-kept short-game area – so much the better. You can personalize one of these schedules and enjoy some quality time out on the range. Those of you who do not have that luxury will just have to be a little more creative in your thinking. That might involve setting out your own targets at various distances, inventing practice games to play on the course, or focusing more heavily on those drills and exercises that can be rehearsed at home, without actually hitting a ball. All of these options are covered inside.

Ideally, find yourself a reputable teaching professional, someone you have confidence in, and invest in a series of lessons. Don't just rely on the advice of your friends, for however sincerely they might pass it on, the old adage remains: 'Amateurs teach amateurs to play like amateurs'. Sound instruction from a qualified instructor will help you to avoid the usual pitfalls and greatly enhance the quality of your practice time and your enjoyment of the game generally.

Like anything worthwhile, you only get out of golf what you are prepared to put into it. There are no short cuts to shooting lower scores, and no substitute for determined hard work. Of course, some want more than others. Five-time US Amateur champion Frank Stranahan hit shots off the decks of the ship that took him to win the British Amateur Championship in 1948. Hollywood superstar Sylvestor Stallone is so bitten by the golfing bug he has been known to practice hitting balls off the side of mountains in between takes.

We are all different. But as challenges go, few come any better than golf, and there is a wonderful enjoyment to be had just hitting balls, being out there alone, working at a game you know you can never beat. That's the thrill. My hope is that through the pages of this book you find within yourself the motivation to improve and properly maintain your game. Not to mention having a lot of fun in the process.

David Leadbetter

DAVID LEADBETTER

◁ *Such is the popularity of the game today that practice facilities and ranges thrive in built-up areas, like this one – slap-bang in the middle of downtown Chicago.*

1

IN SEARCH OF A BETTER GAME

THE MAJORITY OF THE GOLFERS I teach don't need me to tell them how important practice is if they want to do justice to their talent. Many of them came up through junior ranks to be low single-figure players, with designs on one day turning pro; the rest have already made that transition. For them, golf is a serious, often obsessive, business.

What they do need, though, is a sense of *direction*. They need someone to simplify the finer points of good technique and to help them understand their swing and any particular tendencies they have. Someone to make them think a little harder about what makes their game tick, and to help them analyze their performance on the course so that their practice time might be more effectively structured.

Out on the range, the real testing ground, they need a reliable source of feedback to monitor their progress, and a regular diet of practical drills and exercises that help them to capture the sensation of a good swing, and so speed their improvement. This is really what being a teacher is all about, and while we may not be working one-on-one, the thoughts and ideas presented in this book will provide you with the same service and motivation I try to give all my students.

You may not be blessed with the natural ability of a scratch golfer, and you almost certainly don't have as much time as you would like to tinker with your swing and work on the skills that go to make up your game. But if you are committed to becoming a better player, you can make it happen. All it takes is a little common sense and forward thinking. Above anything else, *good golf is a frame of mind*.

Out of interest, I checked with the thesaurus: what is this concept of 'practice' really all about? A number of the given definitions caught my eye: '*drill, exercise, polish, prepare, rehearse, repeat, study* and *train*'. Wonderful words in a golfer's vocabulary. At least they ought to be.

A healthy approach to improving and maintaining your game does not involve beating a few balls every once in a while in the hope of finding something handy for the weekend. Such a hit-and-miss approach leaves too much to chance. You might find something that works one day, but it's gone the next. Without any real thought there is neither rhyme-nor-reason to your practice session, and no consistency in your game.

Contrast this with the habits of the smart player – someone who likes to keep a close track of his performances out on the course. His finger is on the pulse: he knows the strengths and weaknesses that exist in his game, and so he is able to focus on those areas that most need attention, and organize an effective plan of action.

Such a process of analysis and self-evaluation is perhaps the most significant difference between golfers who find themselves stuck in what you might describe as a 'handicap trap', and those who are able to set themselves realistic goals and gradually improve the overall standard of their game. Appraising your game is like appraising a business – you have to look at the facts and figures in black and white, and be entirely rational in your evaluation. But before we look at the ways in which you can do this, let me first identify and explain the three distinct types of practice.

PRACTICE: *Three games in one*

IN ITS FULLEST SENSE, the art of practicing golf embraces a host of related activities, each one designed to help a player prepare fully for his game, both physically and mentally. So that we are clear on exactly what we are dealing with, I am going to suggest that we classify these activities as three distinct levels: (1) the **pre-game warm-up session**, (2) the **technical work-out** on the range, where you deal with the details of your swing, and (3) various **mental rehearsal techniques** that help a player train his mind for the challenges of the course – often referred to as the 'inner game'.

A strong case can also be made for a fourth element of practice, which would involve such matters as keeping fit for golf – the strengthening of specific muscle groups that benefit the swing – and learning how to relax, both on the practice tee and in competition. Just as society as a whole is more aware these days of health and fitness issues (both mental and physical) in terms of improving performance, the modern tour pro makes good use of certain proven techniques and exercises in each of these areas to improve his physical strength and mental resilience. You might regard this as a 'new wave' in golf instruction – we'll look at it in more detail in Chapter 5.

Naturally enough, a rounded strategy of improvement involves striking a balance between all of these elements of practice, though of course every golfer's habits and needs will vary. We are all different in that respect. The determined, single-minded approach Ben Hogan took to the practice tee, famously beating balls until his hands could take no more punishment, is certainly not for everybody.

Back in 1945, in what will surely remain the most phenomenal winning streak in professional golf, the legendary Byron Nelson won a record 11 tournaments in a row on the PGA Tour, and had such a feel for his swing that the only form of practice he participated in was warming up before he played. He was afraid that if he *over*-practiced he might lose the great feel he had. It's interesting to note that throughout his career Byron was a great lover of facts and figures and an assiduous note-taker. He kept detailed records of every game he played, so when he did practice he knew exactly where to direct his efforts.

Such talent is all too rare, and I suspect that your own strategy of improvement will include some quality practice time spent in each of the three categories I have defined above – and probably some experimentation in the fourth.

THE WARM-UP: *Getting ready to play*

Preparing your body to play good golf could well be the most valuable form of practice there is. Stand on the 1st tee cold and you don't give yourself much of a chance to perform to the best of your ability. You may start to play well later on in the round, but over the first few holes your swing will probably remain a mystery, and, as far as your score is concerned, the damage will be well and truly done.

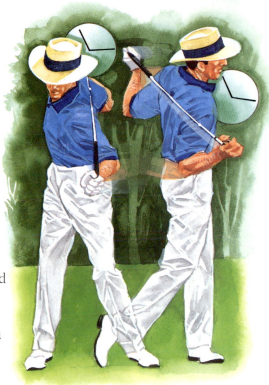

Warming-up is all about limbering up and getting a little feel going before heading for the course. Most of the players I teach devise for themselves a routine that may take anywhere between 20 and 40 minutes to complete. First, spend a couple of minutes stretching your body and warming up the muscles you need to make a good swing. There are various ways of doing this, and as you work through this book you will come across a number of alternatives. But one of the easiest and most effective exercises is the pivot-drill that you see illustrated here.

Take your regular posture, hook a club across your shoulders, and rehearse your pivot motion. Focus on turning your shoulders through 90°, back and through. The key is to maintain your body angles – particularly your spine angle – as you turn and shift your weight into the right thigh, and then back again through 'impact' before straightening to a nice, vertical finish. Repeat this five or ten times. If you lack flexibility, try the following variation on the pivot drill. Place the club behind your back and hook the shaft between your elbows.

Another good loosening exercise involves nothing more complicated than taking hold of two iron clubs and swinging them together in slow motion. Use a basic two-handed grip and get used to the sensation of *swinging the clubhead*; feel the muscles in your arms and torso stretching out like strong bands of elastic.

Once you feel ready and loose
enough to make a swing, hit a few balls. There's
no need to go through every club in the bag. Start with a
wedge or sand iron, pick a target, and try to cluster a handful of balls as
closely together as possible. Then drop down to a 9-iron, 7-iron, and so on.
Ultimately, tee up a few balls with a 3-wood, and then the driver. But don't get carried away
with the longer clubs. There is always a danger you might try to hit the ball too hard, which
can cost you your rhythm before a game. If you ever find yourself in that situation, throttle
back to a short iron, or make a few swings with your feet close together – a useful drill that
will help you to recapture a nice, easy rhythm.

It must be stressed that, this warm-up period is not a time to be working on a swing
change, nor on any other major element in your technique. The best policy is to keep your
thoughts simple, and work on striking the ball with a nice, repetitive tempo. Study the
shape of your shots and be prepared to play with that shape out on the course. That's the
golden rule: if you are fading the ball in practice, then that's what you must play for out on
the course. Don't aim at the flag and scratch your head as the ball drifts right of the target.
Aim *left* of the flag, and let the ball do its thing in the air.

Having warmed up your swing, leave at least ten minutes for some short-game work.
Ideally, you should always try to splash a few bunker shots to get a feel for the weight and

texture of the sand, and chip a few balls until you are in tune with the pace of the greens. Finally, take your putter and hit a few long lag putts from 30 or 40 feet. Sense the rhythm and tempo of your stroke as you *flow* the putter back and through along the line to the hole. Try to run each one tight to the cup. Then knock in a few very short putts to give your confidence a final boost before heading for the tee.

These are the basic skills you should try to cover before you play. If the course doesn't have a practice facility, at least set aside the time to make 20 or 30 rehearsal swings with two or three different clubs to get the feel of the clubhead and to stretch the muscles in your arms, back and shoulders – not least to protect yourself against injury. Alternatively, if there's a decent patch of thick grass in the vicinity of the 1st tee, take a mid-iron and swish the clubhead through the grass – the resistance you meet will heighten your sense of impact, and prepare you to strike a ball.

△ *A comprehensive warm-up routine can be achieved in just 20 to 30 minutes. If you can afford more time than that, don't waste it just beating balls with your driver. Spend it on and around the practice green, polishing your short-game skills. If you can't find the time to warm up, don't be surprised when your engine stalls at the start of the race.*

IN-DEPTH PRACTICE: *Developing, building, refining*

The fascination of this game is that it is always changing. Unfortunately, you cannot plug in a certain swing thought and keep it forever, and never does a course play the same way twice. Golf just isn't that simple. Your game will feel great one day, and the run of the ball will be with you. Then, inexplicably, you lose the thread, and before you know it your luck changes. The old saying *'I've got it, I had it, I lost it!'* just about sums up the frustration this fickle game can muster in all of us.

Ever-changing weather and course conditions further complicate the puzzle. Go out in a gusting wind and your swing will be buffeted to such an extent that your ball-striking is bound to be affected, making some sort of compensation necessary in order to maintain control. The same is true when you play on a particularly hilly course, or switch between a links-style course and a parkland setting. Certain adjustments are required – not only in the way you prepare to strike the ball, but also in the way you visualize your shots and plot your strategy from tee to green.

Your short-game and putting skills are constantly put to the test. One day the sand in the bunkers is wet and firm, the next it is soft and powdery, or the depth of the sand varies. So your bunker technique is constantly under scrutiny, and your feel for splashing the ball out of the sand must be revised and fine-tuned over and over again. This is often the case from one week to the next on tour. While the greens themselves are generally consistent in character, the quality and playability of the sand can vary enormously. Tour players know they must adjust their method to suit the sand, and a good number carry two or three different sand irons with varying degrees of 'bounce' for that very reason.

Most of us tend to play our golf at one home course, but in order to be versatile it is important that you are aware of these possibilities, and be prepared for all eventualities. If you switch from quick greens to a slower surface, your putting stroke may have to reflect that change; where once you stroked your putts, now you have to *hit* them. In America there are quite a few different types of grass to contend with, especially depending on the region or the time of year. So running adjustments are often necessary. Many players experiment with different weights and lofts of putter, depending on the green surface, perhaps favoring a heavier and more lofted putter on a slower surface, for example.

You see how golf teases you. These and many other variables too numerous to list explain the unique complexities the game presents. Indeed for many golfers – especially the better players – adapting to these challenges in practice until they can play all sorts of different shots, in all sorts of different conditions, is the real pull of the game.

To this end, the full-on technical work-out ought to be regarded as a general surgery, during which time you analyze your swing and work on specific approaches to both improve and adapt your skills. This is largely the science of trial and error, utilizing proven principles to educate yourself as a golfer. What you need to do is to employ certain drills that accelerate the learning process and help you get into the groove of a certain move until it becomes habit.

The time this takes will vary, depending not only on your natural talent, but on the quality of your practice techniques and your desire to improve. At first, time may well be a significant factor – don't kid yourself otherwise. But as you work on the mechanics of your swing and gradually feel more comfortable with the changes you make in each and every department of the game, so you will reach the stage where you are able to make running repairs and practice more for what I term 'maintenance' purposes.

Getting together with a good teaching pro can certainly expedite this process, and many of the world's great players have coaches to make their practice more productive. My association with a number of top players has been well documented; other player-coach relationships down the years include Bobby Jones and Stewart Maiden; Jack Nicklaus and long-time mentor Jack Grout; Tom Kite and Harvey Penick, and the latest great young player, Tiger Woods, with Butch Harmon.

MIND-GAMES: *Focus and concentration*

A question I often get asked is whether golf is more of a mental or a physical challenge. It's an interesting point. Ben Hogan probably summed it up best when he said *'Golf is 100% mental and 100% physical'*. These two elements are impossibly entwined.

The levels of stress and anxiety that can threaten a player's focus and concentration will vary and change dramatically as he develops his skills and works his way up the scale as a golfer. For the rank beginner, the swing is just as much a mental as it is a physical problem. His mind is awash with instruction and he tries to juggle too many ideas. While a touring pro might focus on just one or two key swing thoughts to keep his mind focused on the course, I have spoken with amateur players who describe half a dozen (often conflicting) ideas floating around in their head – a problem that inevitably leads to tension, or *'paralysis through analysis',* as the great John Jacobs succinctly describes it.

One of the keys to successful learning is to keep things simple; to focus on just one or two swing keys that enable you to repeat a good motion and strike the ball with some degree of consistency. Not so many that you become bogged down in a haze of technical chaos.

In reality, it is the ability to replicate the ball-striking skills you learn in practice out on the golf course, where every shot counts, that determines your success. In other words, you have to learn to manage your game and deal with the unique mental pressures that spring up the moment you leave the practice area and set foot on the 1st tee.

You often hear commentators describe a certain player as being 'mentally tough', but what does that actually mean? In a nutshell, it refers to a state of what I term *total positive concentration,* the ability to blank out certain external pressures and focus your mind on playing one shot at a time, one hole at a time. Apparently cocooned in a bubble of concentration every time he stood up to the ball, Jack Nicklaus played perhaps the greatest mental game of all. He provides every golfer with the model lesson in perfecting and repeating a sound pre-shot routine, which is by far the most effective protection you can have against pressure. A pre-shot routine helps you to cement the fundamentals of the grip, alignment, stance and posture every time you set up to the ball, so you are more likely to repeat the skills learned in practice out on the course when you need them most. What's more, it gives your mind something positive to work on, and gets you 'target oriented'.

The principle is quite simple: the more you standardize a procedure, the less you have to think about it. Study good players and you will notice that their actions on the course are semi-automatic; the time it takes between first surveying a shot and pulling it off will hardly vary, whether they face a tough tee shot or an easy pitch. This consistency in routine diffuses pressure, thus increasing the odds of a good shot being played.

It's all part of being able to be *focused* on the golf course, but it takes repetition to build these good habits, and you cannot expect a routine to work on the course until you have perfected it in practice.

If we assume a typical iron shot to a green, these are the points you must work on. First, make good use of a yardage book, sprinkler-heads or other markers on the course. Figure out how far you have to carry the ball to the target and make a mental note of any potential trouble. Stand behind the ball and try to absorb the situation. Visualize the shot in your mind's eye, take in the prevailing conditions and consider all of the options.

Once you have decided on your course of action, move in to the ball and go through the motions: aim the leading edge of the club dead on the target, and align your body accordingly. Waggle the clubhead once or twice to keep your hands and arms relaxed, and then pull the trigger. Let the motion *flow* – just as you pictured it. Even on the practice tee, Jack Nicklaus always maintained that he never hit a shot until he had a vivid picture of the flight of the ball in his mind. He described this element of his routine as 'going to the movies', and it's a part of the game you must spend time perfecting. So work on your pre-shot routine in the same way you would work on a certain swing change – practice it until it becomes a natural part of your game.

The quality of your thinking is fundamental to good golf; you must at all times be alert and in-tune with the layout of the hole as you step up to the tee. One of the dangers of playing most of your golf at the same course (as most of us do) is that it's easy to become lazy in your approach. You can avoid that if, every once in a while, you vary the way you play your regular course. Mix things up a little and force yourself to hit a variety of different shots. A fun way of doing this is to limit yourself to teeing off with just a mid- or long-iron on the par-4's and 5's, where normally you would reach for the driver. In so doing you dramatically change the nature of each hole, and so face a host of longer and tougher approach shots to the green. Not only will this force you to think about your club selection, it will test a range of skills you might otherwise not use.

Another good mental exercise is to imagine playing a course you are familiar with on the practice range. Play each hole in natural sequence – hit your tee-shot, second shot, and so on, imagine any hazards that exist – i.e. bunkers, trees and water – and play each shot with full concentration.

I suggest this as a particularly effective routine to players who feel they might be getting a little too technical in their thinking, which was exactly the situation Nick Faldo found himself in during the Masters at Augusta in 1996. So, rather than thinking 'swing', Nick played the course on the practice tee before each tournament round, visualizing each shot and hitting the clubs he knew he would need. That mental exercise soon had him in tune with the conditions, and rarely has he appeared quite so focused as he went on to claim a dramatic victory. More on this technique in Chapter 5.

FACTS & FIGURES: *How does your game shape up?*

NOW THAT WE HAVE touched upon the various types of practice, it's time for you to turn the spotlight on your own game, to discover the specific areas that need attention. I am a firm believer in the keeping and up-dating of certain performance figures, as doing so enables you to set specific goals and to structure a more effective practice schedule.

At this stage I would advise you to take a blank sheet of paper and make a few notes. Think back over the last two or three games you played, and try to identify any patterns that emerged – good and bad. Total up the number of fairways and greens you hit in regulation figures, and note the number of putts you took over the course of a round. Circle those holes that really cost you dear, and identify the shots that caused the trouble.

Did the majority of your poor shots miss to the left or the right of the target? How often and how successfully do you put the ball in play off the tee? Were your shots to the green reaching pin-high, or did they tend to finish short of the hole? When you missed a green, how often did you take the opportunity to get up-and-down?

The short-game analysis will be particularly revealing. Over half of the shots you play in a round of golf are from within 100 yards of the hole, and the lower your handicap, the more critical the short-game has to be regarded in terms of maintaining your performance. Study the numbers. How often do you knock the ball to within 15 feet or so with a wedge in your hands? Assuming a decent lie, what's your conversion rate like from a greenside bunker? And what is your putting average? If you tend to miss a lot of mid-range putts – say, from between 8 and 15 feet – where does the problem lie? Do you tend to pull the ball left of the hole, or push it to the right? Do you generally leave putts short, or charge them by? Do you have trouble getting a good 'read' on the line and pace of the putt?

Amongst these questions are the answers to a better game, and pretty soon you should have in front of you a set of performance notes similar to the example you see over the page, which are typical of the problems experienced by a mid-range handicap player. After a few rounds you will see patterns emerging, and this will direct you toward the aspects of your game that need to be improved, possibly with the help of a teaching professional.

Dig a little deeper. What really costs you in a typical round of golf? If you are one of those golfers who tend to get off to a poor start, then improve as the round progresses, I would be inclined to suggest you are not preparing yourself properly. So you need to make more of an effort to arrive for a game with sufficient time to warm up, as we discussed earlier. Getting off to a good start is the key to putting a decent round of golf together – the first couple of holes you play pretty much set the tone for what is to follow. Much of the anxiety you might suffer over the opening holes can be eliminated with a few minutes' loosening up and establishing a good rhythm, and those 1st-tee nerves can also be controlled quite effectively with the right breathing pattern. The secret is to create a rhythm with your breathing that stabilizes the tempo of your swing. If you feel nervous or tense, take a long, deep breath as you set up to the ball, and then exhale as you waggle the club and prepare to go. As all that tension flows from your body, you will be left feeling calm and relaxed, ready to repeat a good tempo. Try it next time you feel those butterflies in the stomach – the technique works with every club in the bag. Even humming or whistling a tune can help to reduce tension, so important for good golf.

Another problem you might recognize is that of keeping a good score going. A real danger out on the course is to get too far ahead of yourself, thinking about later holes in the round and what might happen to your score. If your tendency is to follow one poor hole with another before you get back on track, then likely as not you are thinking poorly, and inclined to adopt a defensive strategy. To overcome this you must learn to stay in the 'present'; thinking backwards or forwards only results in you losing your grip on the 'right here, right now'.

The irony of this game is that success has little to do with the number of good shots you hit in the course of a round. It's the quality of your 'misses' and the clarity of your thinking that matters most of all, which is why the mental element is so important in terms of your ability to repeat the skills learned in practice out on the course. And any mental errors you do make need to be addressed in just the same way that physical errors need work and attention.

Poor thinking leads to poor decision-making and the poor execution of certain shots, plain and simple. A classic example is taking a driver off the tee when a 3-wood or a long iron is the better option. Your objective is to *get the ball in play*. Do that and you keep the high numbers off the card. Even great drivers of the ball, like Greg Norman, Ernie Els and Tiger Woods, will play the percentage shot.

Remember, the woods are full of long hitters…

Distance control is a particularly important element of good golf. Too many amateurs think they hit the ball farther than they really do, and inflated opinions do more harm than good. Because they once flushed a 6-iron 170 yards through the air, they figure that's their average, and factor it through the bag. Which explains why I frequently see amateurs come up short of the hole, in three-putt country.

Classy players are not interested in how far they can hit a particular club, flat out. On the practice tee they are more concerned with the quality and the consistency of their striking, and work on grouping shots so tightly that balls almost lean against one another, within a certain range. That's my definition of real control, and it's a skill that sets even the pros apart. Someone like Nick Faldo has such an acute awareness of his swing, and strikes the ball with such purity, that he is able to flight his shots with a repeating trajectory, landing balls to the nearest yard or two. Nick Price is another who judges distances with mesmerizing accuracy.

So don't let your ego get in the way of your club selection. The sooner you learn to be realistic out on the course, the quicker you'll start hitting your target. Taking an extra club enables you to play within yourself, and that raises the odds of you hitting the ball better, and straighter.

HOLE	PAR	TEE SHOT	2nd SHOT	3rd SHOT
1	4	driver 242yds RR	GB left	
2	3	4-iron 180yds to 15ft		
3	4	driver 255yds RR	6-iron 150yds RR	8-iron 120yds to green
4	5	driver skied 220yds F	3-wood 225yds F	
5	4	driver pulled 250yds LR	8-iron 120yds short	
6	3	8-iron 135yds left GB		
7	4	driver 260yds RR	7-iron to green 30ft	
8	4	3-wood 220yds FB	6-iron 140yds short	
9	5	driver 260yds trees	wedge to fairway	3-wood 215yds short
10	4	driver 255yds F	4-iron 165yds short	
11	4	3-iron 190yds F	9-iron 120yds to green 20ft	
12	3	5-wood 170yds right GB		
13	5	driver 255yds RR	5-iron 150yds F	wedge 80yds to green
14	4	3-wood 255yds F	5-iron 155yds F short	
15	4	3-wood 220yds F	wedge 105yds to green 10ft	
16	3	4-iron 175yds left GB		
17	5	driver 255yds F	3-wood 205yds RR	9-iron 95yds short
18	4	3-wood 215yds F	7-iron 135yds to green 25ft	

KEY: F – fairway FB – fairway bunker GB – greenside bunker RR – right rough LR – left rough

COMMENTS Too many shots went right especially driver
Poor pitching accuracy / Inconsistent putting / Too many shots short
* NOTE – 3-wood worked well today

Pitch	Chip	Sand	Putts	SCORE
		20ft	2	5
			2	3
			3	6
30ft			2	5
			2	5
20ft		8ft	2	4
			1	3
	15ft		2	5
			1	5
20ft			1	4
15ft			2	4
		6ft	2	4
			3	6
	2ft		1	4
			2	4
		20ft	2	4
	10ft		2	6
			1	3
			(33)	80

COURSE Leadbetter Woods GC
TOURNAMENT Medal
WEATHER Good, Light wind

PAR/S.S.S 72/71
DATE Sept, 97
H/C 10

◁ The keeping and updating of performance figures is invaluable in terms of your ability to target specific areas of weakness, and so make the most of your practice time. It's also a good way to record your golfing career, and as the years go by, you can reflect on past experiences and the progress you have made.

THROUGH THE BAG: *Key skills on test*

RUNNING THROUGH this type of question-and-answer type analysis every now and again will certainly give you something to think about, and I hope some of the ideas I have presented start you thinking about your game in an altogether more professional manner. And, to complement that information, it's not a bad idea every once in a while to put key skills under the microscope in a practical test. When I analyze a player's game I look out for what you might call ' bread-and-butter' skills: driving the ball, iron play, pitching, chipping, basic sand-play and putting. Nothing too fancy, just solid performances in each area.

Create your own skill-testing station – i.e. set out an imaginary fairway between two flags. Hit iron shots to different targets, always be aware of distances, and test yourself on a variety of scoring shots on and around the green. So much the better if you can run through these tests with a friend of similar ability. That way, you open up a new dimension: practice now becomes an exercise in competition, which teaches both of you to cope with pressure.

Let me stress that the performance targets I have suggested over the following pages are nothing more than general guidelines, so don't read too much into the figures. They simply indicate the level of ability I would expect in each handicap group if a player came to see me for a lesson. Only you know your true potential, so be your own best judge.

OFF THE TEE: *In play, or in trouble?*

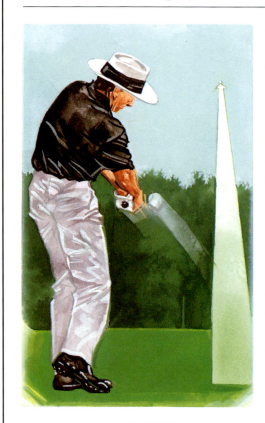

Driving the ball well is a skill you need to develop in order to reach the highest levels of the game, but all too often I find players who struggle off the tee, which suffocates their ability to score.

Take the club you generally like to use off the tee, either a driver or a 3-wood, and imagine a fairway running off into the distance, something in the order of 30 or 40 yards across. Take ten balls and approach each shot just as if you were teeing off in a competition. Remember, the key to consistent scoring is keeping the ball in play – but how many of your tee-shots would have finished in the fairway?

If you can't achieve a success rate of at least 50% with a driver, take it out of your bag. Take away the temptation to use it when it is likely to land you in trouble. Use a 3-wood (or get yourself a driver with more loft) and work on your swing until you can find your target with a significant degree of accuracy.

IRON PLAY: *Consistent flight and trajectory*

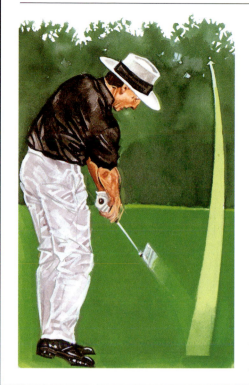

The key with the iron clubs is consistency of flight and trajectory. I suggest you take three clubs – say a 9-iron, 6-iron and 4-iron – and record your ability to produce shots of a consistent shape and trajectory with each one. Again, hit ten balls, and aim to land each one within a certain target area.

Only you know what you are capable of, so set your own agenda. Any shot that finds the green counts as a 'hit'. Compare scores with the three clubs. If you find you score seven out of ten with a 9-iron, but only three out of ten with a 6-iron, then it's pretty clear where your problems lie, and you have your work cut out.

Even for good players, long irons are fairly tough to hit. Unless you are a relatively low-handicap player, say, below a 10, I would strongly advise replacing anything less than a 4-iron with a utility wood. They are easier to hit and give you greater confidence.

PITCHING: *A test of distance control*

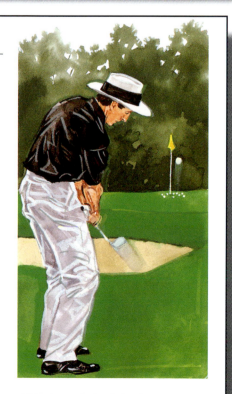

Pace out a typical pitch shot, say to a distance of 50 yards from the pin, and give yourself a good lie. Then, with the emphasis on controlling the distance you fly each shot, pitch ten balls with a wedge or sand wedge. There really are no excuses for missing a green from this range, so all ten balls should find the putting surface. To be considered a reasonable pitcher of the ball, you need to hit at least five of the ten shots to within a 15-foot radius of the hole, and you should be disappointed if any finish outside 20 feet. From 50 yards and in, the single-figure player should be looking to get up-and-down with at least a 50% success rate.

CHIPPING: *The basic 'bump-and-run'*

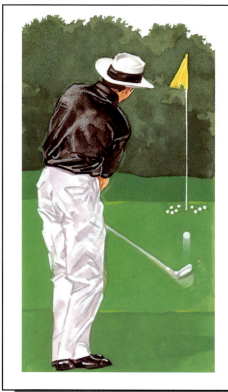

Go to the fringe of the practice green, and, from a reasonable lie, set up a situation in which you have three or four yards of carry to reach the putting surface, and a further ten or fifteen yards to the hole. Use your favorite chipping club, and go through the motions of playing a regular chip-and-run. Visualize the ball landing on a particular spot and releasing to the hole, and try to group all ten balls as tightly as possible. To within four feet can be considered a win.

This is the short game at its most critical. Unless you average chipping *at least* five balls out of ten to within three or four feet of the hole, you're wasting too many valuable shots around the green. If you want to shoot lower scores and head toward single figures, you need to be rolling at least seven balls out of ten to within this distance.

BUNKERS: *The basic splash shot*

Find a regular greenside bunker, and give yourself a perfect lie in the sand. Again, set yourself up to play ten shots in succession to a pin about 30 or 40 feet away, and note the results. Try to stay relaxed, and simply splash the face of your sand iron beneath the ball so that it floats out toward the hole.

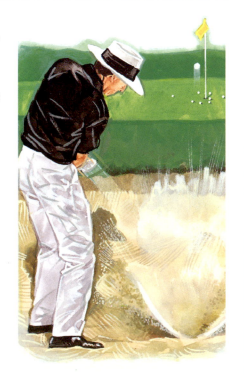

Bunkers cause more problems than they should, so I'm not going to suggest hard and fast figures here. All I shall say at this stage is that every player should expect to escape the sand with one shot and get the ball on the green. In other words, assuming two putts as an average, it should never take you more than three shots to get up and down.

Naturally, the good player sets his sights much higher than that. And rightly so. I would say that a single-figure golfer who is a competent sand player should expect to land at least six of the ten balls within a five-foot radius of the hole, and rarely be outside ten feet.

PUTTING: *Holing the 'money putts'*

Let's start on the green. Find a straight four-footer, and test the accuracy and consistency of your stroke. Have one or two practice putts, then take ten balls, go through your pre-putt routine on each putt, and record your strike rate. Concentrate hard on all of them. On a decent surface there is no reason why every golfer should not look for a success rate of at least 50%. Anything less than that and your putting is in dire need of attention. To be considered a good putter you need to make at least seven out of ten. A low single-figure player should expect to hole at least eight out of ten.

PUTTING: *Rolling the ball 'dead'*

Moving away from the hole to a distance of between 30 and 40 feet, turn your attention to 'lag' putting. The object of the exercise is simply to roll the ball 'dead' into an imaginary two-foot circle (or *'inside the leather'* in old money). Again, take ten balls and focus on both the line and pace of each putt. Go through your routine and feel the ball off the putter-face as you stroke each one toward the hole. Holing out is a bonus.

Whatever your handicap, you ought to be able to lag at least seven balls to within 'gimme' distance. If that proves difficult, then you really do need to spend some time on the putting green. Single-figure players and anyone with serious ambition should score at least nine out of ten.

KEY LESSONS AND PRACTICE TECHNIQUES

M OST CLUB GOLFERS I meet think tour players speak a foreign language on the practice tee. They think there exists some kind of secret technique only the pro gets to know about. Of course, they're mistaken. Week-in and week-out, the great players you see shooting the lights out on TV are working on the mundane stuff out on the range, the run-of-the-mill fundamentals, that hold their game together.

Certainly, the pro wants to maximize the power of his swing. We all dream of that. But unlike most amateur golfers, who would rather skip the more tedious lessons of grip, posture, alignment and so forth, the seasoned player understands that, without a sound foundation, his game is going nowhere. Only with that grounding can you begin to think in terms of hitting the ball better, further and *straighter,* and developing your repertoire of shots. Golf demands that respect.

Whatever your physical capabilities, if you have the determination to succeed, and the discipline to adhere to some ground-rules, there is no reason why you should not develop and groove a swing that gives you the control of the clubface necessary to produce a *repeating* ball flight. Perhaps not a swing that fires the ball at the target every single time (not even the greatest of players achieves that sort of control), but one that certainly narrows the margin between your best and worst shots, and rewards you with a nice pattern. As I see it, many 18 handicappers are probably single-figure handicaps for about 12 holes or so, and drop all their shots on the rest – i.e. the potential is there, but not the consistency. As your bad shots get better, so your scores will get lower. That much is guaranteed. And you stack the odds in your favor when you adhere to the basic principles that shape the swing, and check them on a regular basis.

We are all of a different height, build and temperament, so inevitably these fundamental lessons must be tempered with a degree of individual interpretation. Tall players such as Nick Faldo and Ernie Els have learned and followed the same basic lessons as the shorter players on tour, like Ian Woosnam and Jeff Sluman, but the obvious differences in height and build produce very different styles.

And it's interesting to note that a player's swing closely reflects his personality, too. Just as it should. Ernie Els is one of the more laid-back characters on tour, and swings the club with a slow, lazy tempo. In contrast, Nick Price plays with a style that is altogether more upbeat. But again that beat and tempo is thoroughly consistent, from the tee to the fairway to the green. Keeping all this in mind, simply regard the sequences coming up later on in this chapter as a series of blueprints, if you like, that highlight some of the key positions I believe you need to be aware of and check on a regular basis. But before that, let me clear up one or two well-worn myths that can do your game no good at all.

CLICHÉS THAT HURT YOUR GAME

'KEEP THE LEFT ARM
STRAIGHT'

O N MY TRAVELS around the world I get to see some pretty wacky and unusual interpretations of the golf swing. Some things you just wouldn't believe. But certain problems are all too familiar, and generally stem from an unhealthy diet of myth and folklore, which seems to exist in golf instruction wherever the game is played.

I'd be surprised if you were not familiar with most of these expressions, drawn from a long list: *'Keep your left arm straight in the backswing'; 'Try to make a big turn'; 'Tuck your right elbow in close to the body', 'Drive your legs for power…'* And, of course, the old favorite, *'Keep your head down…'*

Though there may be some truth behind the principles upon which these clichés were originally based, taking them too literally, or out of context, can seriously inhibit your ability to swing the club with a free-flowing motion. Take the business of a straight left arm. If you stand over a ball thinking about keeping your left arm straight in the backswing, you succeed only in creating tension. Your fingers will begin to tighten around the grip, the left arm seizes up, and that muscular gridlock spreads like wild-fire through the upper body. With the odd exception, I can think of very few top players – let alone amateurs – who appear to have an absolutely straight left arm at the top. *Fairly straight,* maybe, but certainly not tense. It's not a feasible swing thought, so don't dwell on it.

A degree of 'play' and softness in the left arm promotes a full backswing and enhances your rhythm. The only place you want your left arm to be firm and straight is at the moment of impact, and this is as a result of centrifugal force pulling on the clubhead.

Tucking the right elbow tight into the side of the body is another fault that ties a player in knots. Anyone who thinks along those lines might just as well slip into a straight-jacket, for as he moves the club away from the ball he severely restricts the width of his backswing arc and ends up with a rather short and powerless jerky action. Again, there is no *fluidity* of motion.

As a matter of interest, this idea of tucking the right elbow in close to the body dates from a time when no self-respecting golfer would have been seen without a waistcoat and tailored jacket, items that clearly tended to restrict the backswing. How times have changed. With modern equipment and the increasing athleticism in the game today, golfers are encouraged to create width by allowing the right elbow to work away from the body. In his prime, everyone said Jack Nicklaus had a 'flying right elbow', but it wouldn't be frowned upon today. And just look at the top of Fred Couples' backswing!

A good backswing is one that involves the upper body turning and coiling against the resistance of the hips and thighs, creating a sort of 'gearing effect' between the lower and upper body. In that way a player creates torque in his swing, and tremendous

'TUCK IN THE RIGHT ELBOW'

power with it. But, under the illusion they are making a BIG turn, I see golfers who turn their body so quickly away from the ball that, by the time the club is only halfway back, they have made a full hip and shoulder turn, requiring independent hand and arm action to get the club to the top of the swing. Without that resistance in the lower body, there is no *coiling* effect, and no real power, either.

'MAKE A BIG TURN'

A point I always make in my teaching is that a good swing demands that you synchronize the component parts, so that the turning of the body and the swinging of the arms are timed to arrive 'in sync' at the top, with a great deal of resistance and coil. The player who misunderstands the concept of the 'turn' usually ends up with a big body action, but no real coil. I'd rather see less turn, and more coil.

Such a fault can also lead to symptoms of a reverse-pivot, in which a player shifts his weight onto his left side as he completes his backswing, then onto his right side as he swings through the ball. In other words, the weight shift is at odds with the momentum of the swing – which makes no sense at all.

Remember, it's important that you synchronize the turning of your body with the swinging of the arms and clubhead. And that turn must coincide with a positive weight shift – i.e. first away from and then toward the target. Like the boxer who 'punches his weight', the golfer must learn to shift his weight into the shot to generate maximum clubhead speed and power.

Incidentally, as long as it does not roll to the outside of the right foot, you can shift your weight laterally into your right side. This is not a sway. You are simply turning your body against the flex in your right knee, and loading up your swing with a good coil.

The notion that you should 'drive the legs for power' is very much a remnant of 1970's teaching, and still a problem that plagues a number of golfers today. But you won't hear too many chiropractors complaining about it: driving the legs forward from the top results in the upper body being so far behind the lower body through impact that a player is forced into using his hands. He generally ends up with a classic reverse-C finish, which puts tremendous strain on the back.

Again, this synchronization between the upper and lower body is what's missing. Yes, the lower body does work hard through the impact area, but it must initially remain calm in the downswing before the hips make an aggressive clearance. It's a matter of timing. You don't want to drive the legs so quickly that the upper body has to play 'catch up'. A good leg action gives you the balance, while your focus must be on stabilizing the swing and rotating your left side through impact. Not sliding through it.

And so to the king of the clichés – 'keep the head still'. This is without doubt the most common and probably most damaging advice in golf. You don't want your head to excessively bob up or down in a vertical plane during the swing, and neither should it rock back and forth toward the ball-to-target line. But there are few good players who do not move their head a little from side to side in the process of turning their

'DRIVE THE LEGS'

body back and through – especially with the longer clubs, and most noticeably with the driver.

Allowing the head to move an inch or two lessens the strain on the spine and enables you to properly contain your weight shift as you wind and unwind your upper body over the hips. I see that as being a positive element in a dynamic and repeating swing, and I encourage it. The golfer who thinks about keeping his head rigidly fixed in place on a full swing denies himself that freedom, and sets himself up to experience the wide-ranging (and often painful) effects of a reverse-pivot.

So you see how these innocent one-liners can hinder your development as a golfer. I want you to understand these clichés and the faults they inevitably breed. Then forget them. These tired expressions get you thinking too much. Worse than that, these so-called tips get you thinking in the wrong direction; they hijack the rhythm of your swing, and dissipate your speed and power before you reach the ball.

So, let's instead focus on the positive keys I look for in a good, repeating method. While advancements in technology enable us to photograph the swing from all angles, and study frames in isolation, it's important that you understand a good swing is not a stop-start series of positions; it is a fluid, continuous motion within which certain common denominators can be identified. That *fluidity* is what all good players have in common.

'KEEP THE HEAD DOWN'

FUNDAMENTAL LESSONS

THIS BOOK WAS NOT designed to include much in the way of theory. My thoughts on the mechanics of the swing are well documented in my first book, *The Golf Swing*, and I stand by them today. However, there are certain principles you simply cannot afford to ignore, and over the following pages I have presented the key thoughts I use in my teaching so that you can at least begin to visualize in your mind the way a good swing takes shape.

Why do we place such emphasis on the basics? Because they are the nuts and bolts of a good method. Adhering to proven principles is what will enable you to avoid common pitfalls and create a repetitive motion. Ultimately, we work on these lessons on the practice ground so that when the time comes to go out and play, we do so with confidence and trust in our swing.

Thinking creates tension. We all know of golfers who think too hard about what they ought to be doing, so much so they get in their own way. What you have to understand is that it's impossible for your body to carry out all the messages your mind sends. In learning this game, you 'train to trust'. Physical practice teaches us muscle memory, and we use it to fine-tune a repeating method. A good golf swing is very much an instinctive action, which allows you to focus your mind on the target, being able to concentrate on the 'where' rather than the 'how'.

Let me stress up front, I don't preach a method, I teach a philosophy. And that philosophy takes into account the human factor. We are all different, and, like fingerprints, no two swings are ever exactly the same. There are certain ideas I relate to the golf swing that suit player A, and others that suit player B. That is to be expected. So regard the following lessons as providing a blue-print, and don't be afraid of personal interpretation, as and when you feel it is appropriate.

THE SET-UP: *Forming your grip*

Good golf begins with a good grip. The way you position your hands on the club pretty much determines the nature of your swing, and there are no excuses for getting it wrong.

(1) *Start with the left hand. Place the club diagonally across your hand, so that it runs just above the base of the little finger, through the crook of the forefinger. Don't get it too high in the palm – a common error that creates tension and results in a lack of mobility in the wrist.*

(2) *As you wrap your fingers around the grip, join the thumb and index finger together. Don't create a gap between the two. Pay attention to the position of the left thumb, also. You don't want to extend the thumb too far down the shaft. Pinch it fairly 'short' on the grip, so the left hand assumes a nice, compact position.*

(3) *Holding the club off the ground, you should see two to three knuckles and a distinct 'cupping' at the back of the left wrist, while the last three fingers anchor the grip. The left hand is now fitted in such a way that the wrist is free to hinge correctly – vital in the process of 'setting' the club in the backswing.*

(4) *As you bring in the right hand, think in terms of it sitting parallel to the left. That's the key to creating a unit. Then, when you close your right hand, the left thumb should be covered, fitting snugly beneath the fleshy pad at the base of the right thumb, with the right index finger and thumb forming a slight trigger.*

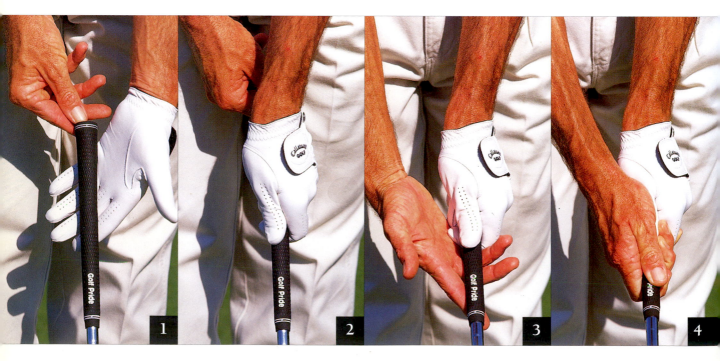

How you choose to join the hands together is a matter of personal preference, and you should experiment with both the interlocking and overlapping styles, the details of which are illustrated here. By quite a margin, the overlap (or Vardon) is the more popular choice on tour, but you must find the grip that suits you.

Ultimately, the test of a good grip is that the two hands work together as a cohesive unit. Waggle the clubhead about (5). Your hands should feel secure, but at the same time mobile. Don't squeeze too hard. A light grip-pressure is important. Tension ruins more shots than anything else. Your hands and arms should feel 'soft' and relaxed – you ought to be able to sense the weight of the head on the end of the shaft, and waggle it about freely.

When you change your grip, be patient with it. Repetition is the key. Work on forming and reforming your grip at home at every opportunity – even in front of the TV. Do it until a good grip becomes a habit.

interlocking grip

overlapping grip

KEY-POINT CHECKLIST

- *Between two and three knuckles are visible on the left hand.*
- *The Vs formed between thumb and forefinger on each hand run fairly parallel, and point between your chin and right shoulder.*
- *The key pressure points are the last three fingers on the left hand, and the right hand on top of the left thumb.*
- *There is a great sense of 'feel' in the triggered right forefinger.*
- *Your hands and arms are 'soft' and relaxed.*

5

THE SET-UP: *How to create good posture*

Posture is important because the swing is in many respects a geometric movement. There are certain angles involved that must be set correctly at address, and then maintained to produce a repeating swing and a controlled ball-flight. Specifically, creating and maintaining a consistent spine angle is one of the keys to repeating a good turn and to swinging the club on the proper plane. It also determines your ability to remain in *balance*, which is vital as you increase your speed through the ball.

This simple routine will help you to create a good posture:
(1) *Stand with your feet shoulder-width apart, toes turned out 20° or 30°, and hands on hips.*
(2) *From here, bend gently from the hips, stick your rear-end out, and flex your knees slightly. Sense a little pressure on your thighs. Finally, let your arms just hang in front of your body.*
(3) *Relax your neck muscles, slide the right hand beneath the left (to the position it would assume on the club) and ease your left hip 'up' so that it is set slightly higher than the right. Check your profile in a mirror.*

The right side of your body should now be in a fairly passive position, which is important for the right-handed player. Your weight should be centered on the balls of your feet, underneath your shoe laces. (You ought to be able to rock back and forth, from the toes to the heels – that indicates good balance.) The lower part of your back should be straight and your chin perked 'up'. This gives you the freedom to turn.

THE SET-UP: *How to guarantee good alignment*

Golfers struggle with matters of alignment for the simple reason that they stand to the side of the ball, which can distort their perception of the target line. The danger is that errors in your alignment can easily go undetected, and if your aim is even slightly awry, you will instinctively build compensations into your swing to start the ball on line. In other words, one fault can easily lead to another.

So pay attention to your alignment as you set up to the ball. The key must always be the position of the clubface. Start your routine by aiming the clubface dead on the target, and let your body take its orders from there. Using the clubface as your guide, set your body on a track *parallel* to that ball-to-target line. Then move in, aim the clubface squarely on the target line, and get your feet, knees, hips, shoulders and eyes to complement one another, all parallel to the ball-to-target line.

It's a good idea to place a couple of clubs on the ground to assist you (inset). That way, you create a conscious awareness of the target line and your body line, which helps you avoid basic errors creeping in.

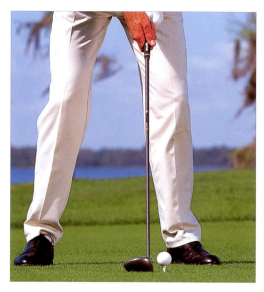

DRIVER

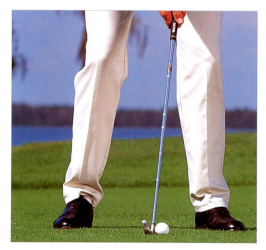

5-IRON

9-IRON

THE SET-UP: *Stance and ball position*

The issue of ball position is one on which players and teachers often have a differing opinion. One school of thought says keep the ball in one position for all clubs, and just vary the width of the stance, which if achievable, is theoretically more consistent. This approach is generally preferred by better players – Johnny Miller, a particularly 'legsy' player, was a fan of this 'one-position' philosophy.

More commonly, though, I find that many players, professionals included, follow the other school of thought, which suggests that the ball is played forward in the stance for the longer clubs (i.e. driver, fairway woods and long irons), a little further back for mid irons, and about in the middle of the feet for the lofted shorter clubs. And while this system may require a little more feel for each shot, it does allow a player to strike down on the ball with the shorter clubs, and deliver a sweeping *ascending* blow with the longer clubs.

Clearly, this is an area that requires a little experimentation. You must find the ball position that allows you to sweep the ball off a tee with the driver, and pinch the ball off the turf with the irons. When you practice, try to get into the habit of periodically rearranging the two clubs on the ground to form a T-shape that enables you to monitor both your alignment and ball position simultaneously.

Whenever you work on the basics of grip, alignment, posture, ball position and so on, any change you make will feel uncomfortable for a while, and it's all too easy to slip back into old, familiar habits. It has ever been thus. As Ben Hogan once said: *'If a grip change feels comfortable, then you haven't made a grip change'* – so stick at it. And the same applies to all the other aspects of the set-up position.

SET-UP: *Things to look out for*

WEAK LEFT-HAND GRIP

If you wear a hole in your glove, look out. That's a sure sign the club is running too high in the palm of your hand, and you need to fix it. Remember, the club should run *diagonally* across the left hand, through the knuckle on the forefinger to the base of the little finger.

ALIGNMENT CLOSED

Because they tend to aim their body before aiming the clubface, many golfers end up in a closed position at address – i.e. they aim to the right of the target. As a result they are forced into compromising their swing in a desperate attempt to start the ball on line. This is why it's so important you stick to the proven procedure: clubface first, then feet, knees, hips and shoulders *parallel to that line*.

ERRANT BALL POSITION

Generally speaking, golfers who slice the ball tend to play it too far forward in the stance, while the hooker is more likely to play it too far back, toward his right foot. If you recognize either of these faults in your own game, make the necessary adjustments.

POSTURE 'TOP-HEAVY'

This is a common fault – the upper body tipped too far forward. Not only does this prevent a good turn being made, it ruins balance. A good posture is a 'tall' posture. Raise yourself up, stand proud and get your chin off your chest. In the correct position, you should be able to rock from toes to heels.

HOW THE BODY WORKS

I BELIEVE THE KEY to building a repeating swing lies in a clear appreciation of the role played by the body, specifically the relationship between the torso and the legs. A good leg action can be seen to provide a steady center of gravity as the torso winds and unwinds, and so helps to stabilize and balance the swing. It's a simple concept.

    The exercise you see here captures the essence of my teaching philosophy, and before we go on to look at the swing in its complete form, I want you to appreciate exactly what the body does. The secret to control is creating momentum with the rotation of the body: a turning motion first to the right, and then to the left, featuring a positive transfer of weight. Let me explain this in more detail with a simple drill.

BODY ACTION: *The engine that drives the swing*

Holding your hands behind your back, feel the balance and poise of a good set-up position (1). From there, feel a slight lateral move to the right as you begin to wind your upper body and gently initiate the transfer of weight across into your right thigh. Establishing that lateral weight shift (what I call a 'bump' to the right) is the key to the first move, whereupon you can really start to wind up the bigger muscles in your upper body, turning the right hip and right shoulder behind you in a clockwise fashion.

    Focus on turning your right shoulder out of the way, while at the same time resisting

this upper-body rotation with some flex in your right knee. You want to get to the point where your chest is on top of the right leg, your back fully turned on the target and your left shoulder comfortably under the chin (**2**).

Having created resistance and coil in the backswing, stretching the muscles in your upper body, you now want to sustain that energy coming down, so that it can be released where it really matters – through the impact area. To do this you must settle your weight in the transition period, and hold your legs steady as you prepare to release the spring. Sense that the left side of your body reverses the momentum: the left knee, left hip and left shoulder pulling away toward the target – in that order (**3**).

The watchword throughout is *patience*. Give yourself time to unwind, and the process will happen almost instinctively. Then, as the left side rotates and clears away, the right side of your body will be free to drive hard through impact, so that you finish with the right shoulder pointing at the target, your knees nicely together, and with the majority of your weight on your left side (**4**).

As you learn to coordinate the rotation of your trunk with the balance and control of a passive leg action, so you will be strengthening the heart of your swing. The result (with a club in your hands) is that you will be better able to utilize your arms and upper body as you rotate through the ball, producing straighter and longer shots.

All good players move their body well. If the body moves correctly, you create a great deal of speed, with the promise of there being good *flow* in your swing. Ideally, you want to feel that the good angles you create at address are maintained pretty much to the point of impact. That way your swing will follow a repeating path.

ARMS, HANDS & CLUB

I DON'T INTEND TO add further comment to the long debate over whether a good body action is more important than a good hand/arm action, or *vice versa*. In terms of your ability to play good golf, the two elements are critical. Neither is much use without the other.

What I will stress is that a good body action breeds consistency. It sets up a free-flowing motion of the clubhead, and enables a player to work with natural centrifugal forces to generate speed and strike the ball. In short, it provides a sound framework within which the hands and arms are able to *feel* the shot and *work* the ball.

Rather like the notion of spinning a weight on the end of a string, a good body action is the hub or engine that controls the swinging of the arms and the club through the provision of centrifugal force. As long as the arms, hands and body work together in sync, a player is able to move the club on a good path and plane, and turn this force into a moment of leverage that enables him to hit long, solid shots.

Problems occur when the arms and the body work independently of one another, which disrupts the radius of the swing and dissipates the centrifugal forces present. As a result, a player has no real control over the shape of his swing, fails to maximize his clubhead speed, and is left to suffer all manner of inconsistencies through impact. So that you can avoid these pitfalls, I want to give you a series of checkpoints that you can use as a guide in building your swing. They will help you harmonize your body, hand and arm action, leaving you with a free-flowing motion.

THE MOVEAWAY: *Coordinate club and body*

Common to every good swing is the coordinated movement of the hands, arms, the club and the body in the first few feet away from the ball, with a rhythm and tempo that pretty much set the tone for what is to follow. These elements can be seen to work 'together' in harmony during what I term the 'moveaway'.

Moving the club, hands, arms and chest as a unit starts the clubhead away low to the ground along the correct inside path – just as geometry would suggest. A good feeling to have here is that, as your left shoulder turns, it pushes the left arm down slightly, so the hands themselves pass close to the right thigh.

On a specific point, notice that while the clubhead travels on a path that is inside the ball-to-target line, it remains *outside* the line of the hands. This is important. You don't want to roll the wrists and whip the club back too much on an inside track, and neither should the hands be seen to work independently of the body, lifting the club abruptly outside the line of the hands.

HALFWAY BACK: *Fully 'set', club on plane*

From the initial moveaway position (and using the line of the original shaft plane at address as a guide) the club should now be 'set' up on a slightly more vertical plane, and this is where you reap the benefit of a good grip, as the wrists are instrumental in 'cocking' or setting the club into the correct position.

The checkpoint to look for in a mirror occurs as the right arm begins to fold and the left arm reaches a position where it is snug across the chest, parallel with the ground. Be aware also that the hands should now appear to be positioned opposite the middle of the chest, while the grip-end of the club should be pointing approximately at a spot just inside the ball-to-target line. You achieve this 'set' position by rotating the left forearm gently away from the ball and hinging the wrists – a slick combination which begins in the moveaway, but which is accelerated as the hands pass from knee to hip height.

Looking face on, the top of your right forearm should just be visible above the left, while the left elbow points down toward the ground. The right elbow is free – not tucked in hard to the side of the body – and you will notice that the flex is retained in the right knee. The legs are braced, fully supporting the coiling motion of the upper body.

Stand and watch a good player hit a few shots and very quickly the halfway back position in his swing stands out as the reason he swings so repetitively. It looks so simple: as the hands reach hip-height the wrists have hinged to set the club on plane, and all that is then required is a good shoulder turn to finish the job off.

HALFWAY BACK: *Things to look out for*

INDEPENDENT HAND ACTION

Allowing the hands and arms to work independently of the body is one sure-fire way to ruin the backswing sequence. Typical symptoms include whipping the club back inside away from the ball (which results in a very flat backswing) and picking the club up abruptly, which leads to a very steep swing plane. Either way, the coordination between club, hands, arms and body is lost, and further manipulation will be required to get the club back on line as the swing progresses, which makes consistency very difficult.

AT THE TOP: *Shoulders turned, clubface 'square'*

From the halfway position, reaching the top is easy: the upper body winds up fully, the left shoulder turns under the chin, and the right elbow supports the club. The chin eases to the right to facilitate a full turn, the majority of body weight is now planted on the right side, and the left arm is relaxed – all vital signs of a sound backswing.

Other specifics to note are that the clubface is parallel to the left forearm (in what we term a neutral position), with the clubshaft approximately parallel with the target line, and that the hands are a reasonable distance from the head, indicating that good width has been maintained throughout. The wrists can be seen to be fully cocked, with the left shoulder under the chin and the back facing the target.

This is a position that owes its correctness to the fundamentals and the early movements in the swing: with a neutral grip and a good set-up position, rotating the shoulders about the natural axis of the spine and allowing the wrists to hinge correctly rewards you with this powerful wound-up position at the top.

AT THE TOP: *Things to look out for*

POOR WEIGHT SHIFT, CLUB OUT OF POSITION

If we consider the rear view, ideally, I expect to see a 90° angle formed at the right elbow, supporting the club in this classic 'waiter's tray' position. When you check your own swing in a mirror, look for this position; you don't want the club pointing either too far left or right of the target. Be alert, also, for any signs of a 'reverse-pivot', a common fault that sees too much weight languishing on the left side as a player completes his backswing.

Remember, a positive weight shift into the right side is the key to a correct and powerful body motion.

STARTING DOWN: *Unwind the spring*

If you can get into a good position at the top, and initiate the downswing sequence correctly, gravity pulls the clubhead back down to the ball and a lot of good things will happen. The arms and hands will follow the recoil movement of the body, and the club will approach the ball on a plane that pretty much matches the shaft angle, as you set it at address. You are now in a position to release the clubhead correctly.

The downswing sequence is very difficult to control with conscious thought. It is largely a reaction to the backswing; any errors you see or feel are likely to be *effect,* rather than cause. Which is why I stress the importance of focusing on the early part of the swing.

It is important that there is a smooth change of direction as the body begins to unwind and the weight shifts gently across to the left side in readiness for impact. The spine angle should be maintained, the right elbow must move down and in front of the right hip, and the club should be on track to approach the ball on an inside path.

STARTING DOWN: *Things to look out for*

'OVER THE TOP', QUICK LOWER BODY

Backswing thoughts are easier than downswing thoughts, because, as I have stated, downswing is the *effect,* and not the cause. But if you do use a video camera and have the ability to freeze-frame the action, you may be able to detect certain faults. Most common would be the right elbow moving too far away from the body, and out toward the target line as you start down – the classic 'over the top' move, resulting in an early release of the club. Another fault (though one that applies mainly to the better player) is that of 'rushing' the weight to the left side too early in the downswing, which results in too much of a slide or a spin-out of the lower body, causing the hands to work excessively through impact.

IMPACT!: *Head behind the ball, clubface square*

As we study the impact position, captured here at speed, let me reiterate the importance of trying to maintain a good spine angle (as determined by your original posture position) until the moment the club meets the ball. The spine angle provides you with a consistent axis about which to turn, and that's what you need in order to produce a repeating swing and to be a consistent ball-striker.

Refer back to the pivot drill earlier in this chapter, and use it to develop this quality in your own body action. Wind and unwind, maintaining that spine angle until impact, whereupon you begin to straighten as you complete your finish to face the target.

Let me stress this point: good players control the rotation of their body to return the hands, arms and clubface pretty much to the position they were in at address, albeit at great speed. The hands themselves are 'quiet' through impact, slightly leading the clubhead through the ball. Note the position of the left hand: it is not buckled, but strong, in control of the clubface. Meanwhile, the head is steady, and the left arm and clubshaft form a straight line momentarily after impact, with the left side of the body firmly braced to absorb the hit.

IMPACT: *Things to look out for*

LOSS OF SPINE ANGLE, BREAKDOWN OF LEFT WRIST

A number of factors can result in a player disrupting his spine angle in the downswing, though one of the most common is a tendency to stand up on the shot in an attempt to scoop the ball into the air, which leads to all manner of inconsistencies at the moment of impact. Such a fault is often accompanied by a breakdown in the wrist action as the hands become excessively active through impact – another source of inconsistency.

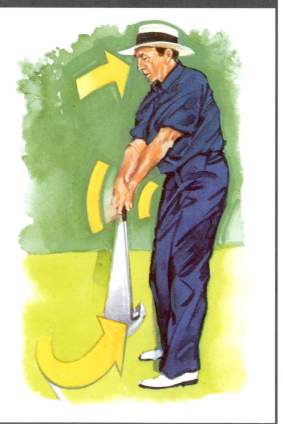

THE FINISH: *Right shoulder to the target*

The way you complete your swing says a lot about your ability as a golfer. Good players rotate freely through the ball to finish with their chest facing slightly left of the target, and their right shoulder pointing to it; their hands finish left of their body, with the club angled across the back of the neck. It's a pose that can be held comfortably for several seconds.

A good follow-through is the culmination of many good things, and again the body controls the show. As the body turns through the shot, centrifugal force swings the clubhead, like the weight on the end of the a piece of string. Then, once the ball has been struck, the club finally releases and the momentum carries you on to a full and proud finish.

When I look at a player making a full swing, I like to see the clubhead accelerate freely to a complete finish, where the force of the acceleration causes the club to recoil back down with the longer clubs. As you can see, the weight is now firmly on the left side and the body is straight, not arched – perfectly poised and in balance.

It's important to finish your swing properly, so work on achieving this finish position. Copy the style of the great players. You won't get it right unless a lot of good things happen in your swing – but working on where you want to end up actually helps you get there.

THE FINISH: *Things to look out for*

POOR ACCELERATION

A short, restricted follow-through suggests *deceleration* through impact, and suggests to me a tendency to hit 'at' the ball, rather than swinging smoothly through it. To counter that problem, commit yourself to accelerating the clubhead all the way to the finish. That will reward you with a full release through the ball, and a complete follow-through, your right shoulder pointing to the target. It will also enhance your acceleration through impact – where speed matters most.

PRACTICE TECHNIQUES: *How to use the video*

ONE OF THE GREAT hurdles to overcome in the process of developing a swing and improving your technique as a golfer is that of separating *'feel'* from reality. What you might think or feel you are doing in your swing, and what actually occurs, are often two very different things. In fact, the hardest thing for a coach is to convince a pupil that something is right when it feels so awkward and out of sync. That is why it is so important to get feedback from a reliable source, the video camera being the most significant learning tool in recent years.

I use video playback as a source of information and feedback to complement regular teaching sessions, though I must add that it is never allowed to take over. And a golfer needs a basic understanding of the swing before he scrutinizes his own method too closely. Otherwise it's easy to get too caught up in technique, complicating what may very well be a simple issue.

If you have the opportunity to use a video, set the tripod at a height that enables you to center the camera on your navel, and focus on recording your swing from each of these three angles:

(1) FRONT VIEW – face-on, directly opposite your hitting position;
(2) SIDE VIEW – looking down the line toward the target;
(3) REAR VIEW – studying your swing from the rear.

The better player might also like to observe his swing from the perspective of the target – i.e. to hit shots back over the camera, which will reveal what's happening through and beyond impact. Just be careful you don't catch the ball thin!

With a mid-iron, take three or four swings from each of the three angles, and zoom in on at least one of these angles to get a closer look at the details of your grip and set-up position. Then replay your swing, first at normal speed, to get a general idea of tempo and rhythm, then in slow-motion, and finally frame-by-frame for close analysis.

Focus on the key positions outlined earlier in this chapter. Down the line, take a good look at the quality of your set-up position, and then follow the sequence from start to finish: moveaway, halfway back, to the top of the swing, impact and follow-through. Concentrate on what the club, hands and arms are doing in relation to your body. Check the plane and path of your swing, and look for continuity of motion.

From face-on, view the body motion to see what the trunk is doing. Check the quality of your turn and leg action, and whether or not you are getting through the shot correctly. Finally, the rear view will give you an excellent perspective of whether or not you are transferring your weight properly, and immediately raises the alarm should you display any tendency to reverse-pivot. You should also be able to determine whether or not you are maintaining the width and radius of your swing, releasing the clubhead correctly and extending to a good finish.

Remember, most problems take root at address, so look closely at your set-up position from all three angles. A poor set-up can cause the arms and the club to get out of position in the early stages of the swing, and when that happens your body will do its best to compensate so that you are able to get the clubface into some sort of square position for impact – in other words, one fault leads to another. This point cannot be overstated: coordinating the movement of the arms and body is the key to a consistent swing, so use the video to determine the point at which that synchronization breaks down.

For example, if the turning of your torso on the backswing is completed by the time your arms are only halfway back, whereupon you lift the club to the top, your swing is out of sync. Ideally, the upper body and arms should complete the motion back at about the same time, thus resulting in better synchronization through impact.

Another benefit of the video is that it enables you to capture your swing on tape when things are going well. Tour players do this to boost their confidence and to reaffirm lessons they are working on – not just for the full swing, but for short-game and putting, too. I advise this practice as a means of storing good images and positive swing thoughts.

Hit a few shots with various clubs and add a commentary to remind yourself of the key swing thoughts you were using at that particular time. You can then refer back to these images and thoughts when you do (inevitably) lose your swing some time down the road. Once you get used to seeing your swing on film, and understand your weaknesses and tendencies, the video will enable you to determine whether or not you are on track as you work toward certain goals. It is also useful in other departments of the game – chipping, putting and bunker play.

One final word of caution. While the video is undoubtedly a most effective source of feedback, it does not suit everybody. If you are fairly satisfied with the quality of your ball-striking, it could well be foolish to start analyzing your swing in any great detail and opening what could be a can of worms. I have been known to tell tour players that the battery in the camera is flat to stop them from looking at their swings on video, particularly at tournaments. As long as they are hitting the ball well, I don't want them getting too technical.

There is no such thing as a perfect swing, so don't set your sights too high or toil aimlessly toward a goal that at best is unrealistic. Your job is to make the most of what you do have. As they say in America: *"If it ain't broke, don't fix it!"*

▷ *World-class players like Nick Faldo use a video to fine-tune their technique and confirm key moves in the swing.*

ONE ON ONE: *The benefits of the 'buddy system'*

The majority of faults that come to my attention have their origin in the set-up position. For example, the ball position creeps forward an inch or so in your stance over a period of time. This in turn disturbs the alignment of your shoulders. Without you actually knowing it, your swing is now destined to be off-line, and, as one thing leads to another, you find yourself struggling to hit the target.

Such faults can be hard to detect yourself, but to someone who knows your game they are more obvious. Which is where the 'buddy system' really scores. Practicing regularly with a friend of similar ability not only keeps your mind alert, but a fellow golfer can help you to check over the fundamentals and monitor the general shape of your swing.

What you need to do is get into a routine of checking the basics: the grip, alignment, posture, ball position and so on. Your buddy can then tell you whether or not you are turning behind the ball correctly, that you have the club on a good plane going back, and that the overall rhythm and flow of your swing is as it should be.

△ *It's in the hole! Short-game competition is the best possible practice to sharpen up your performance in this critical department. Wager a small bet with your buddy, and test your skills under pressure.*

△ *Your buddy can help you to check certain fundamental elements in your swing – such as your grip and set up position, and that you are turning fully in the backswing. And you can return the favor.*

Question him on specific things you might be working on and trying to avoid. For example, is the club moving away low to the ground? Is the clubface open at the top of the swing? Another pair of eyes can help keep your swing on track, and you can return the favor. A friend can also help with motivation. The comment 'great swing' can do wonders for your confidence.

Having someone work out with you in practice also sets up a healthy element of competition. Nominate shots and test your skills, one-on-one. Using piles of six balls, work on something different with each. See who can work the ball with a fade and a draw. Challenge each other to hit between and over trees. Knock down low balls, then hoist them high. Bounce ideas back and forth off each other.

The short-game presents tremendous opportunities to sharpen up your mental edge. Set up a putting competition and test each other to hole out from the critical four-foot range. Create chipping and bunker situations around a green and see who can get up and down most often. Bet something, such as a drink or a ball – anything that keeps you focused and gets your competitive juices flowing. The more often you enter into this sort of competition in practice (in the 'training mode'), the better equipped you will be to respond to real pressure situations when they hit you out on the course.

READING THE SIGNS: *Ball-flight, shot and divot patterns*

Whether I am teaching a world-class professional or a weekend amateur, my job as a coach is to help that player maximize his or her potential by getting them to understand the workings of their swing, and also their personal tendencies which, I might add, generally tend to stay with a player for life. Such an understanding enables a player to work effectively on his game to the point where he is able to strike the ball with a reasonably consistent flight pattern.

When the time comes to add up those numbers on the card, it is the general quality of your ball-striking, and the control you have over the shape and trajectory of your shots, that determine your success. I can stand and talk all day about the mechanics of the swing, but what does the ball do in the air and how consistently are you able to repeat that shape? Some swings may not look pretty, and yet they return the clubface to the ball fairly consistently at impact – and that is really all that counts.

Analyzing the shape and trajectory of your shots is another source of feedback that you need to understand and be aware of. Some would say it is the most important, though I think it is wise to tread carefully here and not be too hasty in making a firm decision. What you see isn't always what you get…

For example, I have worked with good players who hit the ball left of the target and swear they are coming 'over the top'. In fact, they are simply too far *inside* the line approaching impact and so use their hands very aggressively, causing the face to close on impact. But, under the illusion that they are coming over the top, they work on swinging *more* from the inside, and so end up fighting an even greater tendency to hit the ball left.

So it is very important that you interpret the flight correctly, and it's a good idea to back up your theories with the video camera, to see exactly what is happening in your swing. But there's no doubt that the way in which you strike the ball is a valuable guide as to what's actually taking place at the moment of impact, and it pays to be aware of the basic laws of ball-flight.

Here are a few of the clues to look out for:
- Most common of all faults, a **slice** and a **pull** are from the same family, the divot in each case looking left of the target, indicating a path that is approaching the ball too far from the outside and on a plane that is too steep – commonly referred to as 'out to in'. If the clubface is open at the moment of impact, the result is a left-to-right slice; if the clubface is square or closed at impact, the ball is pulled left of the target. Further evidence of this fault is a divot pattern that points to the left of the target and a high proportion of shots being struck weakly off the toe-end of the club.

- Similarly, a **push-shot** and a **hook-shot** are closely related, being the results of an overly shallow angle of attack, and a swing that can be seen to deliver the club on a path that tracks the ball too much from the inside – commonly referred to as 'in to out' swing. If the clubface is square or slightly open at the moment of impact, such a swing results in the ball being pushed or blocked to the right of the target; if the clubface is closed (or is *closing*) on the ball through impact, the result is a hook, or in severe cases a duck-hook.

Either way, the divot pattern in this case will tend to point to the right of the target, and the ball will often be struck toward the heel of the clubface.

- If you hit a lot of high and weak **'pop-up' shots** with the driver or 3-wood off the tee (as witnessed by scuff marks on the top of the club), and achieve no real distance, your downswing angle of attack is far too steep, and you need to work on shallowing the plane of your swing. Remember, with the woods you want to think in terms of *collecting* the ball slightly on the upswing, and sweeping it away.

- **Fat and thin shots** are caused by similar flaws in the swing, and often occur as a result of a player's tendency to want to 'lift' or 'scoop' the ball into the air. Failing to transfer his weight correctly, usually falling back onto his right side in the downswing, the player finds himself struggling to release the club properly as his right arm becomes trapped. When that happens, the low point of the swing arc is destined to be several inches behind the ball, calling for last-minute compensations with the hands – some recover to catch the ball too cleanly (i.e. a thinned shot), while others dig the clubhead into the turf, catching the ball 'fat'.

To cure these common faults, see my simple fixes in Chapter 3.

THE LONG GAME

A TEACHER'S JOB IS TO EDUCATE a player and show him the way forward. Then it's down to the individual. I believe it's important to provide a golfer with a grounding in the basics (as covered in the previous chapter) and to motivate him to such an extent that he takes on the responsibility to work on his game. In practical terms, that involves designing drills and exercises that enable a player to focus on troublesome aspects of the swing and repeat certain moves until they feel more natural. For me, that's the beauty of drills; not only do they spice up your practice time, they accentuate that elusive element of 'feel', and so speed along your improvement.

Many of the students I see at my academies around the world are bemused when I suggest they practice at home without a ball, simply rehearsing their swing and doing drills. Most are under the illusion that constructive practice has to involve beating thousands of balls. On the contrary, I maintain that the majority of golfers would improve their game significantly if only they would set aside a few minutes during the week to run through some carefully chosen exercises at home. Without the anxiety of hitting a ball, it is much easier to focus on the finer points of technique, develop a repeating method and build so-called muscle memory through repetition of good moves.

Practicing at home is a valuable means of improving technique when time is limited or when the weather is too bad to venture out. Winter is a long period of time for a swing to be kept inactive, and doing your homework will keep you in touch with your swing feelings and get you quickly into the groove when you next go out and play.

If you don't have a lot of space, keep a short-shafted club lying around at home, say a 7-iron cut down to just 30 inches long, which any club repair shop can make up for you. If you have a mirror available, so much the better.

Ben Hogan once said: 'There are not enough hours in the day to practice all the shots you need in golf.' And he was probably right. But with clear thinking and a strong commitment, you can transform the way you play this game… if you want it badly enough. That quality of thinking is not just important out on the golf course, plotting strategy and so on. You have to develop the mental ability to replicate your ball-striking skills under pressure, and so the way in which you think about your swing as you hit balls on the practice tee is a key factor here. Let me explain what I mean by this in terms of the way in which you learn.

When you go out to practice, I suggest you hit balls in groups of five or six at a time – like doing repetitions in the gym. To begin a session, hit the first two groups in what we describe as the 'TRAINING' mode. Say you are unhappy with your game and working on something specific in your swing, which involves rehearsing a drill. In the training mode I want you to think about the specific mechanics of that drill as you hit those balls. Hit the first group with, say, a backswing thought, and the second group with a downswing thought. Think clearly about what you are trying to achieve with your swing, and don't concern yourself too much with the outcome of each shot.

Then change your focus. Hit the third group of balls in what we term the 'TRUSTING' mode. Forget about detailed technical thoughts and think in terms of the target, and what you are trying to do with the ball. Focus on a sense of rhythm and tempo in order to produce a swing that will hit the ball toward the target. Try not to think consciously about the mechanics involved – have an awareness of them, certainly, but then let the swing happen. Remember the old saying: *'Trust it and bust it!'*

You can either repeat this sequence over again, or mix it up a little. A variation I like and recommend to my students is to hit five or six balls in the training mode, working on a specific swing thought, and then a couple of shots with their mind really focused on the target (in the trusting mode) to the extent that they go through their pre-shot routine from scratch. That sort of practice is invaluable in terms of applying your skills out on the course.

These distinct modes of learning are important because they help you to make the transition between *learning* a skill and then *repeating* it for real when it matters most – on the course. It all boils down to 'training' and 'trusting'. Training and rehearsing a new move in the swing is a distinct form of learning, but to apply that skill automatically on the course you must learn to trust what you are able to achieve in practice, and have the ability to keep your mind focused, or 'quiet', as you do so.

And therein lies the secret. Quiz a tour player on his mental state when he's producing his best form and he will tell you it just happens, without interference from the mind. All his thoughts are positive: he visualizes the shot and then simply hits it.

Before we look at the drills in detail, a word of caution. Don't make the mistake of believing that the more you practice, the better you will get. Golf is not a science. Practice for too long and you run the risk of losing your focus. We as individuals have varying thresholds to which we are able to sustain concentration and practice effectively – learn to recognize your own.

Part of the skill in learning this game is understanding your own weaknesses and tendencies, and using your practice time wisely. There are only so many hours in a day. When your swing is on track, go to work on your short game. The key is to practice your weaknesses, and not to dwell contentedly on your strengths.

WORKING ON THE RANGE

CREATE THE PERFECT POSTURE:
Set good angles, maintain good angles

The drill you see here is one I use with the players I teach to help them appreciate the sensation of creating good posture every time they set up to the ball. Specifically, it promotes a straight lower back and, with the chin nicely 'up', enables the body to turn about a consistent spine angle.

Take a club, grab the grip with your right hand, the clubhead with your left. Holding it behind your back (as you see illustrated), pull it tight to your body. Feel the clubshaft correspond with your spine angle as you bend gently from the hips, with a little flex in the knees and a sense of firmness in the legs. The lower part of your back should feel taught and straight (even slightly hollowed), while your shoulders must remain relaxed. You don't want your head to be in line with or touching the shaft; relax your neck and let your head ease forward, just so. Doing that adds the finishing touch to a dynamic posture, one that sets you up to make and repeat a good swing.

Another point I would make here is that your torso has to be tilted slightly away from the target. In other words, the right side of the body is set lower than the left, in what we term a *passive* position. Taking a rear view, you don't want your upper body to be too straight up and down, and certainly it should not lean toward the target. Setting the left shoulder (and to a lesser extent the left hip) in a more prominent position is what enables you to get properly behind the ball – a finishing touch gives you the dynamic look of a player about to make a good swing.

SWEEP INTO ACTION... *and start your swing in 'sync'*

A good backswing sees the clubhead move away low to the ground and on a path inside the ball-to-target line as the body turns. To achieve that you must think in terms of your arms, shoulders and the clubhead moving away *together,* to create a one-piece sweeping motion.

To groove this first movement, place a second ball about a foot behind (and a ball's width inside) the ball you intend to hit, and make a conscious effort to knock that second ball away as you draw the club back to start your swing. In one continuous motion, sweep the second ball away, complete your backswing, and unwind through the shot.

With this drill come a number of benefits. Focusing on that second ball eliminates any tendency you might have to either (i) pick the club up, (ii) whip it back on the inside or (iii) take it back outside the line. Your arms and body are instead encouraged to work in sync, as one unit, rewarding you with a sense of width and rhythm – qualities you can then seek to maintain throughout the backswing.

SET, PUMP, AND GO: *Drill your way to a better backswing*

The importance of starting your swing correctly and employing a sound wrist action is about to be revealed. Because, if you can get into this 'set' position halfway back, with the left arm parallel to the ground, the wrists hinged up, and the club on plane, you are all but booked in for a solid backswing. All you need to do from here is turn your shoulders through a full 90° to arrive at a solid position at the top. That is why I believe most of your conscious thought should be directed toward the set-up, and on grooving the first quarter of the swing.

Take a 7-iron, choke down on the grip (that gives you an awareness of the butt-end) and then focus on this position halfway back. As the hands reach hip-height, you want your left arm parallel to the ground, snug across your chest, with the wrists fully cocked. Make sure your hands are opposite the middle of your chest, as you see here, and that the right forearm is just visible above the left, looking at the position face on. The butt-end of the club should point down at an area just inside the ball-to-target line.

Now take it a stage further. From the halfway position, 'pump' the club gently up and down, sensing the control of the torso. Don't just lift your arms up and down, independently of your upper body. The key is to pump the club a short distance with your chest and shoulders in preparation for making a complete backswing.

Talk yourself through it: *'Pump once, twice, and go'*. On the third count, wind it to the top of the backswing and unwind through the shot to the finish. Counting will help to control your rhythm, and turning your body will give you that perfect backswing position. Do this a few times, then hit some balls with the drill.

PLANE AND SIMPLE: *How to check your position at the top*

When I watch a player I look for several key positions, the top of the backswing being one of the more important. Without wishing to go into too much technical detail, a good backswing sees the arms arrive at the top on a slightly steeper plane than that about which the shoulders turn. Looking down the line, I like to see the left arm approximately bisect the angle between a player's head and the tip of his right shoulder, with the club parallel to the target line.

The test you see me demonstrating here is one that will very quickly enable you to keep an eye on the quality of your plane, and is a simple way to check your swing between hitting balls. Take a club, swing to the top, then loosen your grip on the club, and let it fall. The shaft should strike you approximately on the tip of the right shoulder. That's a pretty safe guarantee that your backswing has been made in a good orthodox plane, which I consider a vital element of consistency.

Should the shaft strike you on the head, then your swing is too upright; if it falls behind your body, your swing is too flat. Either way, your arm swing and body turn are out of sync, and some adjustment is necessary. Find a full-length mirror and get those components working together until you can turn and swing on plane on a regular basis. When you find that slot, both the quality and consistency of your ball-striking will improve.

RIGHT-KNEE BRACE DRILL: *Turn, and feel the resistance*

If I had just one key to offer a golfer to focus on, it would be to maintain the flex in the right knee and then wind up against it in the process of building up coil on the backswing. Straightening the right leg, and thus losing resistance in the right side against which to wind up the big muscles, is a fault I see every day. A flexed right knee serves as a brace, inhibits any sway or excess head rotation, and rewards a player with a tremendous feeling of coiling into his right side.

This has everything to do with the principles of 'resistance' and 'leverage' in the swing. To a large extent, the lower body must resist the turning of the upper body. And a flexed right knee is the key to it doing just that.

Take a 7-iron, play the ball in the middle of your stance, and draw your left foot back until the toe of your shoe is level with the heel of the right foot. Then, with the thought of 'sitting' into the right knee, make your backswing and feel the resistance the right knee provides as you wind up the bigger muscles in your torso. (To heighten this sensation, lift your left heel slightly off the ground.)

After one or two dry runs, return to your normal stance and hit balls; focus on achieving the same feeling in the right knee. Doing this drill periodically will give you the feeling of resistance and balance in the lower body, which will enable the large back muscles to really wind up and coil, thereby maximizing your power.

THE CLOSED-STANCE DRILL: *Improve rotation through the ball*

The drill you see here is designed to emphasize the pivotal role of the body, and it will help to improve your timing through the ball as the right side of your body unwinds and releases against what we term a 'firm left side'. Greg Norman – who is not usually a fan of such drills – likes this one as he feels that by doing it he is able to use his right side by rotating through with his upper body as opposed to sliding his legs.

It works like this. With a mid-iron, position the ball in the middle of your stance, then draw your right foot back until the toe of your right shoe is level with the heel of your left. Move a little closer to the ball, as well. Remember, doing this should only affect the alignment of your feet. Though your stance is now severely closed, your hips, shoulders and eye-line should still remain parallel to the target line.

Making a full backswing should now be a relatively straightforward affair (a closed stance positively assists you in turning your right side away from the target), but it's through the downswing that the real benefits of this exercise are felt. First, swinging upon this closed stance enables you to experience fully the sensation of hitting against that 'firm left side' we often talk about. And, with the left side of your body resisting the 'hit', the right side can really get into the action and rip through the ball. Second, as your upper body learns to

unwind correctly, the club will be encouraged to approach the ball on a much better path. The result is a square clubface through impact, and a more consistent flight-pattern.

Let's take it from the top. Having turned your upper body away from the target, you now want to sense that the lateral motion of your left side and the downward motion of your arms occurs in tandem, while your right foot, knee and hip remain in place for a split second. Once you have made this transition, the whole right side of your body has the green light to free-wheel through impact, and you should sense your chest rotating open through the ball.

The closed-stance drill helps to stabilize the lower body, and so encourages you to unwind 'in sync'. If the left side clears out of the way too quickly (which we term 'spinning out of the shot') the right side will often 'hang back', and is unable to deliver its full power.

Remember, to get the bigger muscles in the body working to good effect through the ball (i.e. the right hip and right shoulder and chest rotating at speed toward the target) there has to be a certain resistance present in the left side – and that's exactly what this drill will teach you. I recommend it particularly for players who hook the ball, where the club is swinging too much from in-to-out and the divots look right of the target. This drill will help to get the club moving from inside-to-square-to-inside as your hands pass close to your left leg through impact.

FORWARD, THEN BACK:
Training a better momentum

Golf is not like other ball-sports, in which your movements are reactionary. Because the ball is stationary, you have to create rhythm and tempo in a golf swing from the very start, and one way to work on this in practice is to extend the club a few feet forwards and begin your swing from there. Simply let it flow back and continue in a single motion to complete your swing and then on to strike the ball.

Good tempo is a common currency among good players, and this running start will help you to find and develop a tempo that repeats itself through the bag. Hit shots doing this. Simply let the club sweep back over the ball and build on that flowing momentum as you collect the ball on the downswing.

On the matter of rhythm and balance, another drill that springs to mind is to hit shots out of a fairway bunker, but without the benefit of shuffling your feet into the sand. A lot of tour players swear by this drill. Take a mid-iron, and work on turning your upper body over a passive leg action. You have to be exact if you are to strike the ball cleanly; any excess lower body movement will cause you to mishit the shot. Sam Snead used to take off his shoes and hit balls barefoot to achieve the same results. And no one swung any better or struck the ball any sweeter than he did.

RELEASE THE RIGHT SIDE
... *and sweep the ball toward the target*

An excellent all-round drill for all golfers is to learn to hit a few shots with the right arm only, using a short iron. This helps in a number of ways: (**1**) swinging with the right arm provides you with a good feeling of the right side turning out of the way on the backswing; (**2**) it can help you to focus on the important position of the right arm at the top; and (**3**) it gives you a good feeling of straightening and 'releasing' the right arm as you swing through toward the target, with the club approaching the ball on the proper angle and plane – especially effective for a slicer.

Take a 9-iron, tee up a few balls, and aim to clip them one by one. In the backswing, focus on achieving a solid and wide position at the top, as your right arm supports the club with that classic L-shape at the elbow. (When you first rehearse this, use your left hand to support the right elbow in a good position). Then, as you begin to unwind, think in terms of swinging in a side-arm fashion, which, in effect, will shallow the plane of your swing as the right arm straightens and releases the clubhead through the ball to a full-flowing finish.

As your confidence grows you will gradually build up speed and find that you can release the right hand and forearm quite aggressively through the ball. The better you get at this, the greater will be the width in your downswing, and the better you will strike the ball.

This really is a great way of training that change of direction, so that you unwind your arm and body in sync, and *swing* from the top, rather than hitting 'at' the ball too early. Nick Price uses this drill on a regular basis, and is quite incredible with it, flighting perfect shots with a touch of draw. He likes it because, being left-handed, it heightens his awareness of his right-side motion.

A SENSE OF IMPACT: *Train for it, then do it*

I am going to suggest two 'impact' drills. One can be rehearsed out on the range, hitting balls. The other, which I will discuss later, is to be worked on at home, where you can reinforce the sensation of achieving a good, on-line impact position.

On the range, taking a moment to reflect on exactly what you are trying to achieve at impact can be an extremely useful way of cementing other ideas you might be working on. So, every now and again, make a slow-motion swing and stop the clubface at the ball to assume a good impact position – i.e. with the majority of your weight on the left side, right knee kicked in, your hips opening up to the target, left arm straight, and hands ahead of the clubhead (above left).

The key to this exercise is then to use this assumed impact position as your starting point. Swing the club back in a normal fashion, and hit some shots, trying to duplicate that sense of impact (above right and inset). I think you'll find that this drill greatly enhances your awareness of what a good impact position feels like, which should increase your chances of repeating it more often.

SUN AND SHADOW: *Rotate body, turn behind the ball*

Here's a neat trick that will help you monitor the quality of your body action. As you see demonstrated here, it involves using the shadow cast by the sun to check your position at the top of the swing, and specifically to see that you are turning fully behind the ball.

For this to work, you need to stand square on to the sun, and place a ball on the ground to correspond with the center of your chest as you look down at your shadow. That ball then becomes your marker as you make your swing, the key being that you rotate your upper body fully behind that ball as you coil to the top.

What you must remember is that, unless you turn and shift your weight fully *behind* the ball in the backswing, you are never truly able to get *through* the ball in the downswing. You have to 'load-up' before you can properly unwind, and this exercise will confirm whether or not you are actually getting behind the ball in the first place.

So, with an awareness of that ball on the ground, emphasize the coiling of your upper body over a stable leg action, and wind up those big muscles. As you reach the top, glance down at your shadow to check that you have turned fully, and that your weight is now loaded on to your right side. And don't worry if your head moves a little to accommodate that turn – your chest should be over the top of your right leg, your left knee pointed in, and your shadow to the right of the ball.

Players who lack flexibility can help themselves here by simply adjusting their stance, and turning the toe of the right foot out a few degrees at address. Flaring the right foot assists you in turning the right side of your body out of the way in the backswing, and so enables you to achieve this fully loaded position behind the ball.

HOMEWORK

TRAIN WITH A WEIGHTED CLUB: *Improve strength and flexibility*

The benefits of swinging a weighted club have long been appreciated by the world's finest players, most of whom exercise on a regular basis to keep their body and golf swing in good shape. There are many training devices on the market these days, but you have to go a long way to find anything better suited to strengthening your golfing muscles.

A wood is something of a rare commodity these days, but if you can find an old wooden club, take off the sole plate and have some lead poured into the head. Your club pro or repair shop should be able to do this for you, and they can also advise you on the weight you need. Alternatively, get yourself a specially designed weighted bar, like the one I am using here.

Once equipped, it's important that you start slowly and build up the number of repetitions. Swing the club slowly at first, gradually building speed. With the extra weight, you will become very aware of the key positions in the swing. By including this exercise in your program, you will notice a tremendous difference in your sense of the swing and control of the clubhead. As you strengthen and stretch out your muscles, so you will enhance your ability to make a full turn and realize your true potential for generating speed and distance.

PRESS FOR IMPACT... *and feel the forces at work*

This is similar to the outdoor impact drill we discussed earlier, but with the benefit of very real resistance. We know the impact position is just a fleeting moment in the swing, but you can duplicate the sensation of impact quite easily, and so learn to appreciate the relationship between certain muscles in your body as the clubface is delivered at speed to the back of the ball.

Take a mid-iron, and find yourself a doorway, or a corner of a wall, that allows you to recreate impact, as you see demonstrated here. Hold the club with your regular grip, assume a good posture, and simply press the clubface hard into the corner of the doorway, making sure the leading edge is square to the direction of pressure. Hold that isometric position for a few seconds and absorb the sensation of impact.

There are a number of points to be aware of. First, the back of your left hand should be flat, pulling the clubface through the ball, as it were. Your hips should be open in relation to the supposed target, and your upper body also needs to be slightly rotated in that direction, exerting force down through the arms and hands. This is where your power comes from: you'll feel tremendous pressure as your left arm and chest tighten together, with the bigger muscles in the torso straining to deliver the clubface squarely on the ball. Stabilizing the 'hit', your legs should be firm, the left side of your body braced, right knee kinked in toward the target, and head behind the ball. Relax, and repeat the exercise for 10 reps.

The most significant lesson to be learned here is that, in order to generate a considerable force, you need to use the bigger muscles in the torso, turning against the resistance of the frame in the direction of the target. This is exactly what happens in a good swing: the rotary action of the body controls the show. Go in search of this feeling when you play for real.

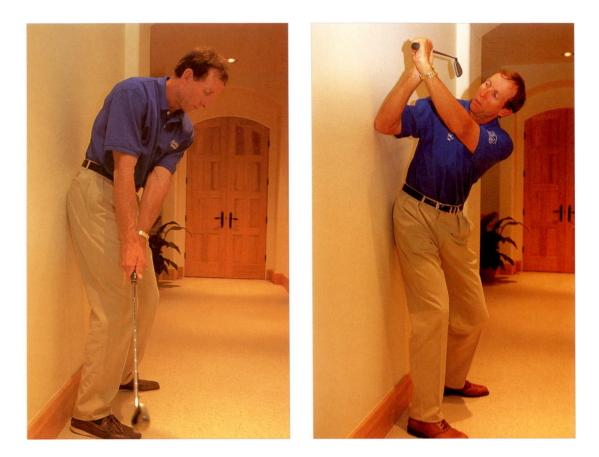

BACK AGAINST THE WALL: *Learn to swing 'in' and then 'up'*

A number of good players sense that the left arm is their guiding arm in the swing. In the process of creating a backswing, they keep a check on the path of the left arm as it describes a radius away from the ball and continues on its way to achieve a consistent position at the top.

That awareness can help you, too. Standing with your back to a wall, take up your posture so that your rear rests against the wall, and give yourself sufficient room to make a backswing. Then, as you rehearse your swing, the key is to feel that your left arm works across your chest, so that your hands head in and up toward the wall. As the hands approach about hip-height, simply let your arms swing up the wall to complete the backswing.

Compare your position to the one you see here. At the top, your right elbow should rest gently against the wall to support the club in a perfect position. The club should lie between the wall and your head. You don't want to clatter the clubhead into the wall as you take it back, or push the hands away from your body to avoid the wall. Simply let your hands and arms work 'in' slightly and then 'up' to get the club into this familiar 'slot' at the top.

The key to the exercise is to track the path of your hands and arms as you rehearse this 'in and up' movement until you can get your right elbow brushing the wall at the top, and the club parallel to it. This drill will give you great awareness of the route the hands must follow to get to the top.

MIRROR, MIRROR: *Reap the benefit of instant feedback*

Working in front of a full-length mirror at home enables you to check that what you feel you are doing and what is actually happening are one and the same thing. You can use the mirror when practicing some of the aforementioned drills and exercises to make regular checks on the correctness of your set-up position, both face on and from the side. Make sure your angles are in order, and that your body is geared up to make a good swing.

Looking down the target line, you can check the quality of your alignment, and monitor the path and plane of your swing as you run through the key positions I demonstrated in Chapter 2: the moveaway, setting the wrists, at the top, starting down, and so on.

I would encourage you also to swing toward the mirror, to see how your body unwinds through the impact area. Coming into the ball, you want to see the left side of your body turning out of the way as your hips, chest and shoulders open up to the target, clearing the way for the hands and arms to release the club through the ball. Look for those images in the mirror, and feel the way your body works as you unwind all the way to a full finish. In that final position, your hands should be seen to arrive comfortably behind your head, your shoulders should be fairly level, and your knees nicely together. Your weight should be solidly on the left side, balanced on the upturned toe of the right foot. Work on your swing until it meets these criteria.

PUSH-PALM DRILL: *For a real sense of stretch & resistance*

Having assumed your regular posture, with a nice flex in the knees, place the back of your right hand against the back of your left, as you see illustrated below. You are now ready for the push-palm drill, a simple exercise in stretch and resistance.

The key here is to sense resistance in the left side and left arm as the right side pulls away to make the backswing movement. Feel the pressure as your right shoulder turns away and the right hand pulls the left arm tight across your chest. As long as you keep things fairly quiet below the waist, you will sense a distinct winding up of the torso and achieve a real extension of the left arm at the top of your relatively compact backswing.

Hold this position for a few seconds; *feel* the opposing forces at work.

Now, as you reverse momentum from the top, and start the downswing, sense that your left hand does the pulling, while your right side resists the change of direction, at least momentarily. I want you to feel that separation as your left side pulls back toward the target – your left knee, hip and shoulder leading the way. Complete this transition successfully, and your arms and hands will fall naturally into the downswing slot. As you continue to unwind, your body will rotate toward the target as the arms straighten through impact – the left side now pulling the right side of your body around toward the target.

Rehearsed properly, this really is a most dynamic and effective drill for a true sense of *coil* and *resistance*. I suggest you do it slowly, and repeat certain moves (such as *stretching* to the top, and changing direction into the downswing) to fully appreciate the good it can do. This drill can be used before a round or practice session as an invigorating warm-up and stretching exercise.

SPLIT-HANDS FOR WIDTH… *and feel key positions in the swing*

A good grip is designed to allow two hands to work as one. But every now and again it makes good sense to isolate the hands on the club to monitor the way in which your arms work in the process of making a good swing. And that's exactly where this drill comes in.

With a mid-iron, split your hands on the grip as you see here (left). Slide your right hand down the shaft until the two hands are about an inch or two apart, but maintain an orthodox hold with each. Now experiment with your swing. Immediately, you will be aware of a heightened sense of feel in both hands, and, as you work through key positions, the role of the arms will be accentuated, individually. I find this drill particularly effective for highlighting the hinging of the wrists as the arms reach waist-height, and also to identify the correct position of the arms and the club at the top of the swing.

It is better if you rehearse this in front of a mirror. Look for that 'setting' of the wrists as the hands pass the knees and reach hip-height, and feel the way in which your left arm works across the chest. At the top, you want to see the wrists properly hinged, the right elbow in a supportive position, and the clubshaft parallel to the target. Then, as you unwind to make the downswing, you should sense that the left arm and shoulder is pulling the club down toward the ball, while at the same time the right wrist retains the angle in readiness for impact. You therefore eliminate any tendency to release the club too early.

SIMPLE FIXES FOR COMMON FAULTS

NOW THAT WE HAVE covered some of the most effective drills that I suggest to players who want to work on improving their swing, let's now turn our attention to what's happening to the ball, and to curing some of golf's most troublesome shots: the slice, the hook, fat shots, topped shots and shanks (the dreaded 's-shot') and a loss of distance with the driver. At some time or other these faults frustrate every golfer, but in my experience they can be eliminated with the help of one or two well-chosen drills. Again, these drills work because they can give you the proper feeling for a certain move, or series of moves, and these feelings are 'internalized' and remembered. In other words, they speed along muscle memory.

THE SLOPE DRILL: *Cures all known hooks and slices*

Creating the right feeling for the swing plane and path coming down toward impact is one of the keys to consistent golf, which is why the two related drills you see illustrated here are so important and universally applicable. Let me explain how they can help you to eradicate those common evils – Mr Slice and Mr Hook.

Anyone who habitually slices the ball does so because the club approaches impact at a severely steep angle, and from out-to-in across the line of play. I touched upon this in the previous chapter, and I know many of you will be familiar with the symptoms: a fairly weak shot, and a divot-pattern that points left of the target. At some time or other, it's a fault that has frustrated anyone who ever picked up a golf club.

To work on eliminating this problem, find a slope that enables you to hit shots with the ball positioned several inches above the level of your feet (see sequence below). This will have the desired effect of *shallowing* the plane of your swing, as it forces you to rotate your

body and swing the club in a more rounded fashion, and so promotes a more natural inside path back to the ball. As you become more proficient, imagine the toe-end of the club turning over the heel through impact, with your forearms providing that 'snap' of acceleration at the vital moment.

There really is no better exercise for the golfer who struggles with a slice. All you have to do is concentrate on your rhythm, and let the slope be your guide. Regular spells of this type of practice will revolutionize your body action and help you to flight your shots with right-to-left draw-spin. Out on the course you can achieve the same sensations if you hold the clubhead a couple of feet above the ground to make your practice swings.

If you are prone to hooking the ball, your needs are totally the opposite. Those raking right-to-left shots are the result of having the club approaching the ball from too far *behind* your body on an overly inside path and on too shallow a plane – faults usually accompanied by a rolling hand action that turns the clubface over through impact. To counter these tendencies, you need to work on hitting shots with the ball positioned a few inches below the level of your feet (see sequence above), to promote a slightly steeper swing and a less pronounced in-to-out path through impact. Again, the beauty of this drill is that it acquaints you with the proper sensations you need in order to get the club swinging on the correct path and plane.

Playing the ball below the level of your feet will also encourage your hands to pass much closer to your left thigh through impact, and to continue on, working *left* of the target, as they should. That's the key to curing a hook: it should feel as though you are sliding the clubface across the ball to create left-to-right spin. Who knows, with a little work you might even cultivate a pretty fade.

SLICING OR HOOKING? *Try these other key thoughts*

If you are slicing the ball, move your hands in a clockwise fashion on the club – i.e. strengthen your grip – hold the club more in the fingers of each hand and lighten your grip pressure. If you hook the ball, do the opposite: try weakening your grip, moving your hands slightly to the left on the club as you look down upon your grip. Also, take the club more in the palm of your left hand, which will help to keep your hand action 'quiet' through impact.

▽ Here's a drastic measure to cure the really stubborn slice. Aiming your body 90° right of your target, position the ball to the left of your left foot, and try to make what will obviously be a very exaggerated inside-to-out swing in relation to your true target. Focus on really releasing the right hand and right forearm through impact. This should produce a shot that has a tremendous amount of hook-spin on it, and acquaint you with the feeling of the club swinging from *inside* the target line, with a full and unrestricted release of the hands. Try to maintain these same sensations as you gradually work your way back to a normal, square position. **WARNING** – Don't do this if there are others near by!

◁ If you slice the ball, focus on rotating your left arm more aggressively through the impact area, so that you turn the face of your watch down to the ground.

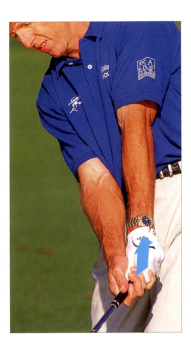

▷ If you are prone to hooking the ball, feel the fingernails on your right hand point up toward the sky through impact, thus eliminating a tendency to roll the clubface closed.

IF YOU PUSH...

Generally speaking, the push-shot is the result of a player moving ahead of the ball through impact – i.e. the body moves and slides *toward* the target and the path of the swing is blocked. A quick fix in this situation is simply to focus on keeping your chin behind the ball as you unwind from the top, and to sense the toe-end of the club passing the heel through impact. This will enable your arms and hands to release the club correctly and start the ball on line.

IF YOU PULL...

Pulling the ball left of the target with an 'over-the-top' type swing is infuriating, because more often than not the ball is struck very solidly and flies further than anticipated as a result of the closing clubface. One way to eliminate pulled shots is to sense that, having made your backswing, your upper body remains turned away from the target as your arms and hands begin the downswing movement. If you can achieve that for a split second, your right elbow will work down toward the right hip, and as the body then unwinds through the ball, the club will approach impact on the proper inside track to produce true and straight shots.

DRIVER:
Lack of distance, pop-up shots

If you set up to hit a driver in the same way you set up to hit an iron, don't be surprised if you struggle to achieve much distance, or hit a lot of weak, pop-up shots off the tee. While a slightly descending angle of approach is ideal to pinch iron shots crisply off the turf, taking a slight divot, the driver demands to be delivered with a sweeping, ascending motion (and no turf contact). If you see ball-marks appearing on the top of your driver, then you are guilty of this fault.

The adjustments that need to be made to hit your driver solidly are quite simple – the set-up is the key. First, settle your feet at least shoulder-width apart, for balance. Second, play the ball forward in your stance, opposite the inside of your left heel, and let your hands assume a position slightly behind the ball. Third, make sure that the majority of your weight favors your right side – say 60%. Your right side needs to be set down lower, almost as if you were swinging up a slope. All this encourages you to catch the ball on the upswing, which promotes a shot with great penetration, a lot of carry and roll – and, of course, more distance.

FAT & THIN? *Improve angle of swing on downslope*

If you are prone to catching the ball fat or thin – and these faults are closely related – take a short iron, find yourself a nice downhill lie, and, with the ball back in your stance, work on swinging the club *down the slope* until you can get the clubface solidly onto the ball. The downslope will encourage you to chase and extend through the ball, with your weight moving well into your left side through impact – qualities which, until now, will have been lacking in your swing.

In tandem with this drill, try to get the feeling that your right elbow is approaching the ball in front of your right hip, and not behind it. That will help you to free-up your downswing, and get your right arm to straighten and release as it should. Remember, also, the importance of maintaining your spine angle to the point of impact – you don't want to stand up or come out of the shot, so keep that flex in the knees constant, and 'stay down' with it.

THE SHANK: *Reverse the loop in your swing*

Without doubt the most demoralizing shot in golf, the shank occurs as a result of the ball being struck out of the hosel of the iron, up close to the shaft, causing the ball to fly at an acute angle, right of the target. This is due to a player's hands being farther from their body at impact than they were originally at address, thus pushing the club outwards. In my experience, some players falsely analyze this shot as the ball coming off the toe-end of the club, which is not the case, and others, who are aware of catching the ball in the corner of the club, attempt to cure the problem by standing further from the ball at address, which only exacerbates the fault.

If you ever suffer a case of the shanks, try this cure. Stand a little closer to the ball, and address it right out of the neck, as you see here. Then, having made your backswing, make a conscious effort to drop the club down on the inside, and sense that your hands pass very close to your body through impact as you attempt to strike the ball off the toe-end of the club. In other words, reverse the loop in your swing. Think about keeping your weight more on your heels, too. This exercise will correct the path of your swing, and after a while, when the S's disappear, you will have the confidence to swing normally.

SHORT-GAME TREASURE

HAVE YOU EVER TAKEN a moment to glance through the performance figures of the leading tour players? The various 'Top-10' categories you find listed in golfing journals make fascinating reading, and confirm what I know is a widely held suspicion among club players: these modern pros really *do* play a different game.

Driving averages in excess of 270 yards are common nowadays, and your average tour player expects to hit somewhere in the region of 75% of fairways and greens in regulation figures. When they do miss a green, they invariably get 'up-and-down' in two shots to save par, or pick up a birdie on the longer holes. Most telling of all, the leading money-winners breeze round in about 27 or 28 putts.

So high is the general standard of ball-striking on the various circuits around the world that tournaments are won and lost on and around the green. Come the post mortem, those great shots are quickly forgotten if the short game is not up to scratch. This only reinforces this inescapable truth: *It doesn't matter how well or how far you hit it, golf is about one thing and one thing only – getting the ball in the hole.*

Press conferences get to the heart of the matter. When a tour player is quizzed on his round, the conversation inevitably turns to a putting dialogue, to details of saves made and opportunities missed. When you play for a living, these are the figures that count. Simply, the short-game skills are very much the barometer of success.

Not everyone has the natural or physical talent to swing and strike the ball like a pro. But every golfer has the potential to improve the quality of his short game, and thus save himself many handfuls of shots in a typical round. Putting, chipping, pitching, sand-play – these skills are not dependent on any kind of exceptional ability. You don't need the physique of a Greg Norman nor the mind of a Nick Faldo to achieve good results. What you do need is a grounding in sound technique, and the desire to shoot lower scores.

Instant reward – that's what we're talking about here. Any time you can set aside for practicing and improving your performance on and around the green will take numbers off the bottom line. And the more accomplished your play from 80 or 90 yards and in, the more strokes you will save, and the lower you will score. Guaranteed.

Calculate the savings you would make if you averaged only a modest 30 or 32 putts per round, for example. This is the target I would set the mid- to low-handicap player. To achieve that might involve you working not only on your putting stroke but also on your chipping method, so that you create more realistic opportunities to get up and down. These skills are related; improving one facet of your short game will generally help along another.

Though it's been said before, it's worth repeating: a player with a sharp, short game and a hot putter is a match for anyone. Nothing is more demoralizing for an opponent (and better for your confidence) than holing good putts and repeatedly getting 'up and down', or turning three shots into two, around the green.

There's another benefit, too. Having that confidence in your ability from short range puts a shine on your entire game. The player who is confident with the putter, one who is not afraid of facing those four-footers, is likely to hole more than his share of mid- to long-range putts, for the simple reason that he is more inclined to 'have a go' at the hole and put a positive roll on the ball. Confidence breeds confidence. By the same token, the player who believes he can get up and down from anywhere is more likely to play a little more boldly from tee to green, safe in the knowledge that his touch and imagination will get him out of jail.

Imagination – that's the key and the theme to this chapter. The short game tests your creative flair. Do you have the ability to invent shots? Are you versatile, and willing to experiment in the search for new tricks that can help you escape trouble? At the core of every good short game is a vivid imagination. You need to 'see' shots before you play them, and have the presence of mind to read situations and gauge the reaction of the ball on the green. Get these elements right and the execution of the shot is largely academic.

It all boils down to repetition, and, just as great short-game exponents such as Seve Ballesteros and Phil Mickelson have worked for thousands of hours on mastering their art, so you must be prepared to go out and practice to gain real benefits. The only way you are ever going to know how the ball responds off the clubface, flies through the air and runs on the green is through making the same basic swing time after time, and carefully noting the results. Such repetition breeds *feel* and, ultimately, great confidence.

Reading a situation, 'seeing' the shot unfold and choosing your club accordingly forms the basis of a good short-game strategy, and it's important that you experiment with a span of clubs to understand the relationship between trajectory, spin and the 'release' on the green that different lofts will give you. The straighter the face of the club, the less the ball will fly and the more it will want to run, and *vice versa*.

Take three of four chipping clubs, a putter and a handful of balls, and spend the odd evening around the practice green to improve your sense of feel and general awareness. Practice with and against a friend; introduce that element of competition to sharpen your focus and test your nerve. Create challenges and set each other targets. There is no better way for the determined golfer to spend his or her time.

PUTTING: *A most imperfect science*

EVEN ON THE TRUEST of greens, and with the purest of strokes, nothing is certain in putting. In the course of his experiments, the short-game exponent Dave Pelz has discovered that a machine that can be set up to repeat a technically perfect stroke will make only six or seven putts out of ten from a distance of six feet on a tournament-prepared surface. Pelz's work highlights the effect tiny imperfections on the green can and do have on the behavior of the ball – what you might describe as 'spike and heel-mark' uncertainty – to which the golfer must add his own fallibility. The human element is such that you cannot realistically expect to make the same exact stroke over and over again.

Be that as it may, putting remains the key to shooting low scores, and the ability to hole putts can turn a good round into a great round, and save a poor ball-striking day with a reasonable score. And you tip the odds in your favor when you follow certain key principles on the green – both mechanical and mental.

Broken down into its basic components, putting is all about *line* and *pace*. These elements are inversely related, and before we go on to look in detail at the mechanics of a good stroke, it's interesting to note that, in the course of his experiments, Pelz found the ideal pace of a putt to be that which would take the ball 17 inches past the hole (should you miss) on any given surface. At that pace, says Pelz, the ball is rolling at a speed that enables it to hug the surface of the green with sufficient overspin to hold its line to the hole. However, there are some great putters who wish the ball to die into the hole on its last roll. They figure that, at a dying pace, the ball has a chance of dropping in should it touch any part of the hole. The game of putting is – and always will be – open to all sorts of interpretation.

Let's examine some of the basic rules that good putters follow in the process of developing and maintaining a sound putting stroke.

PUTTING PRINCIPLES *Grip, posture, alignment and stroke*

If you consider yourself to be a reasonably good putter, but rely chiefly on feel for club and ball, rather than on the specific mechanics of your stroke, then do nothing – why tinker with a winning formula? (It could well be argued that Ben Crenshaw's putting mechanics are not technically perfect – but his feel is second to none.) If, however, your putting is prone to bouts of inconsistency – either the short putts or long lag putts – and you feel you ought to do better, then it's time to sit down and review the fundamentals.

A good putting stroke involves synchronizing the rocking of the shoulders and the swinging of the arms – just like a full swing – but with virtually no wrist action. I like to focus on the triangle formed between the shoulders and the arms; these elements of the stroke must work *together,* so that the triangle remains more or less intact as the putter moves back and forth in a pendulum fashion. Any independent movement in the smaller muscles in the hands and wrists leads to inconsistency, and renders a stroke fallible under pressure. That is why the long-shafted putter is becoming popular these days – it's a pure pendulum motion with no hand action. So basically, as with the full swing, the quality of your grip and set-up position is fundamental to the outcome.

Take the club in the palm of your left hand.

Grip it snug, resting your thumb on top of the shaft.

Keep palms parallel as you introduce the right hand.

THE GRIP: The grip should be made in such a way that the palms are opposing each other on the club, with the hands joined together so that they can work as a cohesive unit. The most common style is known as the 'reverse-overlap', in which the forefinger of the left hand is draped across the fingers of the right (illustrated). That provides a great sense of security, generally, and helps to keep the left wrist locked.

Whether you adopt this style, or a variation of it, prefer a traditional Vardon grip, or even experiment with the reverse-handed method, make sure that you maintain a light grip-pressure, so the arms and shoulders remain nice and 'soft', and you retain a sense of feel. Pay particular attention to the feedback you receive through the thumb-pads on the grip; they promise a tremendous sense of feel and direction.

The quality of your grip is important in terms of the hands working together as one unit, and a useful tip that will encourage this quality in your stroke involves nothing more than adjusting the position of your left hand on the club. Take hold of the putter in such a way that the grip fits high in the palm of your left hand. Run it snug beneath the fleshy pad of the left thumb, and feel the security of that hold as you then close your fingers around the grip. You should now barely be able to see a knuckle when you hold the club up. This 'palm-grip' will assist you in keeping the left wrist firm and flat (and the putter-face square) throughout the stroke, and I strongly recommend it.

THE SET-UP POSITION: Look around and you'll see dozens of individual styles on the putting green – open stance, closed stance, crouched, upright and so on. But for sheer simplicity and function, I suggest you try to stand relatively tall, with your body lines approximately parallel to the line of the putt. Echoing the pre-shot routine we followed for a full swing, start with the careful alignment of the putter-face, and let your body take its orders from there. Naturally, the putter-face should be aimed squarely along the intended line of your putt. As simple as this may sound, I see too many players who suffer poor alignment, so have a friend stand behind you and check your aim on a regular basis.

Check to see that your eyes are directly over the ball (this is accomplished easily if you drop a ball from the bridge of your nose), and let your hands hang *beneath* the shoulders. I like to see the elbows comfortably apart, the inner part of each arm resting on the upper part of the chest. That 'connection' serves a valuable purpose. It enables you to keep the arms and the body working together for the good of the stroke.

There are no hard and fast rules on the width of stance. Suffice to say it should be comfortable and promote a stable lower body, with the knees just a little flexed. Your posture then enables you to control the workings of the stroke with the upper body, rocking the shoulders and swinging the arms back and forth over a solid foundation.

Finally, play the ball forward of center in your stance, so you sense that you catch it on the upstroke, which sets it rolling 'end over end', with a certain overspin that hugs the surface of the green.

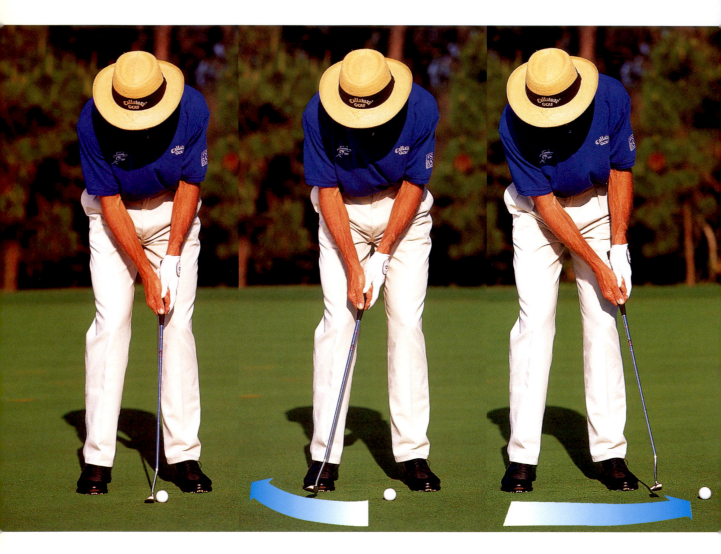

THE STROKE: A good putting stroke should follow a logical symmetry, given the fact that the ball is positioned outside the line of the shoulders and away from the body. My personal feeling is that the putter moves back and through on a fairly straight line for short putts (up to five or six feet) before moving increasingly inside the ball-to-target line on the way back as the putts and the stroke get longer. Returning square at impact, the putter is then seen to swing straight through to the hole before turning slightly inside the line once more.

Controlled once again by the bigger muscles of the shoulders, the hands, arms and putter should be seen to operate together as a unit. A simple reminder many tour players use is: *'Right shoulder back, left shoulder up'*. It's worth repeating these words as you practice. Think of the right shoulder moving 'back' to set your stroke in motion, then the left shoulder moving 'up' as you accelerate through the ball.

Follow these guidelines and the putter will glide back and through on a consistent path – just like a regular swing. Remember, the fewer moving parts, the better and more reliable your stroke will be.

As this pendulum-type action becomes automatic, turn your attention to the overall rhythm and tempo of your stroke, and the pace at which you strike the ball. The golden rule here is that the length of the stroke controls the length of the putt, and a useful exercise in that regard is simply to place tees at 10, 20 and 30 feet and putt to them at random to develop your feel for distance.

Adjust the length of your stroke to meet the length of the putt, and work on repeating a smart 'one-two' beat. You will find a light grip pressure works wonders here for the overall tempo of your stroke – feel the putter in your fingers, and create that 'one-two' rhythm. Just be sure that the length of your follow-through is at least the length of your backswing.

To be sure, try using a musical metronome, and discover the tempo that best suits you as an individual. We are all different. Some players like to swing the putter with a fairly brisk 'one-two' beat; others are inclined to work on a more relaxed, slower beat 'one-and-two'. That is for you to find out. Generally, your putting stroke should match your personality and full-swing tempo.

PUTTING DRILLS: *Blending mechanics and feel*

In creating a short-game schedule, I suggest you consider four specific elements of putting practice: (1) short, 'must-make' putts of up to four, five or six feet; (2) intermediate putts of between six and twenty feet; (3) longer 'lag' putts of over thirty feet, working primarily on feel and pace, and (4) middle distance breaking putts, to discover the correlation between line and pace. As you focus on these skills, and spend time working on the following drills, don't overlook the benefit of putting to a tee. Taking away the pressure of the hole – and *holing* putts – allows you to focus more effectively on matters of technique.

TRAINING A ROCK-SOLID STROKE:
'Rock the shoulders, swing the arms'

Inconsistencies in a putting stroke occur as a player loses the all-important coordination between his arms and body, just as we see in the full swing. In the short term, it might be possible to compensate with independent hand action, feeling your way back to the ball and steering putts, though such remedies are never reliable, and they never last.

To recapture the sensation of a coordinated pendulum action, trap a clubshaft under your arms, as you see here, to get a feeling for that triangular relationship, and focus on repeating a stroke, with a real sense of the arms and shoulders working together. Simply rock your shoulders and let your stroke run on automatic.

Many of the players I teach talk of controlling their stroke with a slight turning of the stomach and chest, which produces a compact and coordinated movement of the arms, hands and putter, and ensures that the shoulders do not rock too vertically, but rather turn round the axis of their spine, as set at address.

Work from short range – say, six or eight feet. As you set up to the ball, make sure that both your shoulders and the shaft are parallel with the line to the hole, then focus on rocking your shoulders and swinging the putter back and forth to that monotonous 'one-two' tempo. Keep your head steady, your grip-pressure light, and listen for that wonderful noise as the ball rattles into the cup.

HOLING OUT:
'One-two...and in'

Short putts are all about *confidence*. The more you hole, the easier they become. There are many ways of practicing your technique, one of the most effective being simply to work around a hole, placing balls in a circle at a distance of two or three feet, and knocking them all in.

Alternatively, you can add a little spice when you play against a friend by introducing a 'draw-back' clause. This forces you both to draw any missed putts back a putter-length, thus eliminating 'gimmes' and testing your stroke on those crucial four-footers.

The key is to focus on rhythm. Don't get caught up in technique. Make sure your set-up and alignment are right, as we discussed earlier, and then repeat that 'one-two' tempo as you stroke each putt into the hole. Practice with your eyes closed, or looking at the hole, to get focused on the putt rather than the putter. Making twenty short putts of two feet in length on the practice green before a round can do wonders for your confidence. Don't stand there and line up a bunch of ten-footers – miss them and you dent your confidence. You want the feel and sensation of repeatedly knocking putts into the hole. That's the way to eliminate doubt and build confidence. And there's nothing sweeter than hearing the ball rattle around at the bottom of the cup.

LAG PUTTING: *Swing the right arm only*

Based on the assumption that most right-handed golfers sense and feel distance with their right hand, another excellent drill is to practice stroking long putts with the right hand only. This immediately heightens your sense of feel for the putter-head, and quickly rewards you with a fine control of distance. Hit four or five balls with the right hand, then revert to your normal putting grip and continue to cluster balls around the hole with a regular stroke. Naturally, a left-handed player would practice with his left hand only.

One of the US tour players I work with, Mike Hulbert, has played a number of tournaments putting with his right hand only. Quite successfully, too.

DEALING WITH 'BREAK': *Mark the borrow, and hit it*

Whenever you face a breaking putt there's a bargain to be struck between line and pace; hit the ball too hard, and it won't take the borrow; baby a putt, and it will fail to hold its line. Naturally, the speed of the green has everything to do with the amount of break you have to play. This is not something you learn through the pages of a book. You have to experience many different types of green and play in all sorts of conditions to be fully in tune with the fickle nature of putting.

But remember the wisdom of the great South African, Bobby Locke, who simplified the issue when he said: 'Every putt is a straight putt'. Your job is to study the line, visualize the ball on that route to the hole, and gauge the appropriate 'break-point', or intermediate target. That then becomes your focus, and you take aim on that point.

To further understand this principle, find a decent breaking putt, hit a couple of test balls, and then place a tee an inch or so above the apex of the line to the hole, as you see illustrated.

Now your objective is to set up squarely to that marker, and aim to hit putts just inside the tee. In other words, you must focus on hitting a straight putt. Judge the pace correctly, and watch as the ball follows the contours of the green to break toward the hole. Use this drill to familiarize yourself with the relationship between line and pace, and to discipline yourself in the art of identifying that all-important intermediate target. Work on left-to-right and right-to-left breaking putts, and also on double-breakers.

Get a routine going. Crouch behind the ball, have a good look at the contours on the green, and make a couple of practice strokes. Pick out your break-point, visualize the line the putt will take, take your aim, and settle over the ball. Take one or two final peeps at the hole, visualize the putt in your mind once again, then let your stroke run free. Ideally, your timing should be such that you repeat a routine similar to this every time you step up to putt.

PUTTING: *Things to look out for*

GET A GOOD ROLL

One of the toughest problems amateurs face is that of swinging the putter across the line of the putt on an out-to-in path, which results in cut-spin and prevents them rolling the ball correctly. You can check the quality of your stroke easily if you mark a circle around the ball (or practice with a range ball), set the line on the ball to agree with the line to the hole, and hit a few putts. If your stroke is true, the line on the ball will appear to roll end over end; if not, it will wobble off-center – a sure sign of a 'cutty' stroke that needs urgent attention.

DON'T PEAK ON SHORT ONES

The 'yips' – the disease that affects players on short putts – is often caused by peeking and moving during the stroke. Move your head to follow the line of the ball and you run the risk of disrupting the alignment of your stroke. Balance and stability are vital ingredients of a good putting action, and it's important that you keep your body still and your head steady until the ball is well on its way. As a rule of thumb, any time you can see the hole in your peripheral vision (obviously a shortish putt), resist the temptation to look up. Try to focus on a spot on the green where the ball was lying until you hear it drop...

CHIPPING: *A test of feel and imagination*

I LIKE TO DEFINE A CHIP-SHOT as one that spends more time on the ground than it does in the air. It is but an extension of a long putt, introducing a certain element of loft on the clubface that will carry the ball over any rough or fringe grass, whereupon it 'releases' and runs to the hole. There's an art to reading a chip-shot, and, like solving a puzzle, great satisfaction to be had when you land the ball on your chosen spot and watch the shot unfold, just as you had imagined.

Great chippers of the ball – and Germany's superstar Bernhard Langer is one of the finest I have seen – will tell you that it's easier to judge and control shots that are rolling on the green, as opposed to flying through the air. Which is why I believe good short-game strategy must involve a range of clubs (to produce shots of varying pace and trajectory), and a mind-set that seeks to get the ball on the green and running on line at the hole as quickly as possible.

There are exceptions to any rule. Some players cultivate their short game with a favorite chipping club, and pull it out of the bag at every given opportunity. Take the great Seve Ballesteros. Wherever possible, he has always preferred to use a nine-iron for chipping, and is a magician with it, sensing distance to the hole and varying the amount of bite and run with a great hand-action.

My feeling is that every player should get used to at least two chipping clubs – say, a 9-iron or wedge for short to intermediate shots, and a 7- or 8-iron to run the ball that little bit farther. To be consistent, I feel this is a good strategy to follow, learning to make one basic swing, and simply changing your club to meet different situations. Controlling the ball off the clubface, and judging the speed at which it rolls – that's what good chipping is all about. Let me show you how to achieve this.

THE GRIP: As with the putting stroke, you really want to keep wrist action to a minimum when chipping the ball. The hands and wrists play an important role in a good chipping method, but excessive wrist-action only leads to inconsistency. For a standard chip-shot you have the option of using either your regular full-swing grip or your putting grip, whichever feels the more comfortable. Whatever you decide, for that extra control it's a good idea to grip a little down the shaft, while a light grip pressure will again enhance your overall feel for the stroke.

THE SET-UP: The chipping stance is created by making minor adjustments to the set-up position I employed with the putter. Notice that my weight now favors the left side. The ball is played back, opposite the right toe, and my hands have eased forward. 'Ball back, hands forward, weight forward' – there it is in a nutshell. Though we shall invite body action, there is no real weight shift involved, so work around a fairly narrow and slightly open stance, with your chest ahead of the ball.

The latter point is particularly important. Leaning toward the target and easing your chest ahead of the ball encourages your hands to lead the clubhead and enables you to have a slight descending blow on your chip shots and keep the ball under strict control.

THE STROKE: Now you are correctly set up, let the pendulum theory take over: gently rock the shoulders and let the hands and arms respond to their motion. As a result of this momentum there will be a slight hinging in your wrists as you change direction and the full weight of the clubhead is felt. This 'lag' effect, as it should properly be termed, is an involuntary element of the stroke, but one that must be cultivated to add that silky-smooth quality common to all good chipping actions.

What we are looking for is a controlled body motion, the hands essentially passive. The triangle formed between arms and shoulders moves in conjunction with the slight turning of the torso, and the key, as you turn through, is that the hands return to the position they held at address. There is no breakdown in the wrist action, and the left hand can be seen to remain in control through impact as the club collects the ball with a slightly descending blow, pinching it off the turf.

Another sign of a well-executed chipping stroke is a follow-through that is a little shorter than the backswing, which reflects control and acceleration through impact. Make a note, also, that the feet remain flat on the ground for balance. There is no real weight transfer involved, just a slight turning of the body, the measured swinging of the arms, and the smooth transition from backswing to through-swing. Executed with grace and rhythm, this close coordination enables you to control the flight of the ball and its subsequent behavior on the green.

One last key: be sure to keep your eye on the back of the ball.

TARGET PRACTICE: *Get a feel for landing distance*

Naturally enough, the straighter the face of the club you are using, the flatter will be the trajectory of the shot and the more the ball will be inclined to run on the green. The question is, exactly what sort of results can you expect with each individual club?

This drill will go a long way toward teaching you the relationship between flight and overall distance. Place a tee in the ground, two or three yards onto the putting surface. This marks your landing point. Then, using a selection of clubs, say, from a sand-iron to a 6-iron, aim to make the same length and pace of swing, and try to land one ball after another as close as you can to that marker. Note the results.

The beauty of this exercise is that it will make you aware of the many different types of shot you can play with individual clubs. The more-lofted irons produce high-flying shots that land and stop fairly quickly, while the straighter-faced clubs produce a lower trajectory and encourage the ball to run that bit farther on the green.

The key to a controlled chipping game is having this ability to get a clear picture of your landing distance to the nearest foot or so, and to understand the reaction you are likely to get thereafter with each individual club. So work on this drill regularly, and enhance both your control of the ball and your imagination in reading the situation.

FLIGHT & RUN: *Learning about club selection*

Once you have acquainted yourself with the basic technique, the way forward is to experiment with a range of clubs and note the results. Try to make consistent contact, focus on repeating the same simple swing over and over again, and see how the ball flies and 'releases' on the green. In so doing you will develop a fine sense of awareness, and gradually piece together a system of club selection.

Naturally enough, the straighter-faced clubs (5-iron, 6-iron and 7-iron) produce relatively low shots and encourage the ball to 'run out' considerably on the green, though of course you must always take into account ground conditions and the speed of the greens. The more lofted irons (8-iron, 9-iron, wedge and sand iron) produce respectively higher-flying chips that tend to check and roll more slowly and thus travel a shorter distance on the green.

PRE-SET IMPACT: *Ball back, hands forward, weight forward*

A problem many people have around the green is that of trying to lift the ball into the air, rather than hitting down and through the shot, as you must, and trusting the loft on the clubface to do its job.

To get around that problem, a useful drill is to practice hitting shots with your right heel up off the ground. That promotes a feeling of being slightly forward of the ball through impact, as if you were playing off a downhill lie (which in itself is not a bad way to practice and develop the knack for playing these shots).

Adopt your regular chipping position, with a narrow and open stance, and ease your weight onto your left side. Steady yourself on the toe of your right foot. You should now feel that the majority of your weight is supported on your left leg, where it remains throughout your stroke. Then, controlling your momentum with a slight turning of the shoulders and stomach in tandem, let your arms swing back and forth to create a smooth and simple stroke. Make sure your hands are firm in leading the clubhead through the ball to deliver a slightly descending blow.

As your chipping becomes more and more consistent, all you have to worry about is where you need to land the ball so that it hops forward on line and releases to the hole.

WRISTY ACTION

Particularly on short chip-shots, there has been a trend toward tour players adopting a putting type grip, for the simple reason that it helps to guard against excessive wrist action. Any breakdown of the hand-action through impact renders a stroke volatile, and makes it all but impossible to judge landing distance and roll. One way to combat this is either to employ your usual putting grip, or simply to weaken your left hand grip, turning the hand counter-clockwise on the club and running it high in the palm of the hand.

Another thought is to focus on making a relatively short follow-through, with the hands leading the clubhead as you arrive at the finish. That will encourage you to accelerate through the shot, but deny your hands the opportunity to get too involved and 'flip' at the ball.

BALL TOO FAR FORWARD

If you can learn to set up to the ball correctly, the basic chipping action can become a fairly automatic one. Problems arise when some element of the set-up is out of sync, and the ball position is often the culprit. In order to achieve that slightly descending angle of strike that pinches the ball smartly off the turf, it is vital that you stand a little open, with your hands and weight forward, and ball back in your stance. If you are standing too square to the target line, and the ball is too far forward in your stance, you are more likely to 'scoop' it into the air, resulting in topped, fat and generally poorly struck chip-shots.

PITCHING: *Compact arm and body motion*

CHIP SHOTS SPEND MORE time on the ground than they do in the air; pitch shots do the opposite. From 30 or 40 yards, and up to a full wedge range of around 100 yards or so, pitching the ball involves using some form of lofted wedge, and producing a shot that flies virtually up to the hole-side, where it bites and stops relatively quickly, with only a little roll.

For my money, this is one of the most satisfying and rewarding shots in golf. A good wedge player can enjoy the sensation of being in touch with the action: he is close enough to the green to visualize and see the shot in its entirety; he can feel the ball off the clubface; and he can see it spinning in the air as it homes in on the flag.

Good wedge players have the ability to control the distance they land the ball. They do this with a compact method that features a close working relationship of the arms and body. In other words, the stroke is well 'linked' together, so the speed and angle of delivery through impact can be controlled and measured with supreme accuracy.

Controlled body, passive hands – these words should tick over in your mind as you practice. Don't be fooled into lifting the ball into the air with too much hand-and-wrist action – the obvious fault of the less accomplished player. Keep your hands 'soft' and passive while letting your swing be governed by the turning motion of your body, and you will find that you are able to pitch the ball with exceptional control.

THE GRIP: Essentially a 'mini-swing', a good pitching method demands that you employ your orthodox full-swing grip. I would stress again the importance of a light, sensitive grip-pressure, one that will enable you to really feel the clubhead and hinge your wrists correctly. You should also consider gripping an inch or so down the shaft to further enhance your sense of distance control, especially on the really short ones.

THE SET-UP: The key to being a good pitcher of the ball is to set up to the shot in such a manner that your address position promotes a nicely synchronized arm and body motion, and preempts impact. To that end it is vital that your body is open to the line of play (your feet, knees and hips more so than the shoulders). Your weight should favor your left side, and the ball should be positioned in the middle of a fairly narrow stance at address. Think in terms of easing your knees and hips into the shot. With your knees flexed and your body comfortably balanced, you should find that your arms hang naturally to place your hands a touch ahead of the ball. You are now ready to make a controlled swing.

When you practice, play around with the ball position, the width of your stance, and the extent to which you open your stance, according to the length and trajectory of the shot you want to play. These are the variables you can and must juggle to be truly versatile.

THE ACTION: In setting the swing in motion, think in terms of turning your chest first away from and then toward the target, and simply let your arms and hands swing in response to the momentum that this creates. Turn slowly, and swing smoothly. What you are creating is a mini-swing: the arms and body work together, while the wrists respond and hinge freely to set the club on a good plane, and provide that essential fluency of motion. So that you accelerate nicely through the shot, make your through-swing at least the length of your backswing.

When hitting shots, the key is to sense a really solid strike, where you clip the turf with the clubhead, taking a nice shallow divot. There is very little weight-shift involved; what you are trying to create is a simple 'turn back and turn through' type of motion – a direct swing that sees the club move up and down on a relatively straight line.

Let me stress the importance of accelerating the clubhead through the ball. You must never decelerate into impact, or make a short swing and then accelerate erratically. Try to

keep the cup angle at the back of the right wrist throughout the shot, especially on shorter pitches – this will ensure that there is no breakdown through impact. A good way to maintain your tempo and control your acceleration through the ball is to think about matching the length of your backswing with the length of your follow-through. Using a clockface analogy, you might work on swinging from 10 o'clock to 2 o'clock, or, to play a fuller shot, from 11 o'clock to 1 o'clock.

In tandem with this you can also vary the speed of your body-action to control the distance you fly the ball. I call this the 'speedometer principle'. Increasing or decreasing the speed at which you rotate your body through impact is the key to fine-tuning distance control. When you practice, imagine you fly a pitch of 50 yards with a 50mph swing; 60 yards would call for a 60mph swing, and so on. As you will discover, varying the speed of your body motion will automatically control the length of your swing. With practice, your judgement of distance will become increasingly instinctive.

DISTANCE CONTROL: *Get your wedge-play measured*

Once you have mastered the basic technique, it's a question of practicing until you can control the flight of the ball with the length of your swing, and working out your 'best' distance with each of your specialist pitching clubs.

Most pros today carry a three-wedge system – i.e. PW (49° loft), sand-wedge (56° loft) and lob wedge (60° loft). To be properly equipped you should do the same. With a range of lofts and bounce, modern wedges are designed to help you cover every eventuality on the course, and enable you to work on repeating a relatively full swing to produce shots of varying height and distance.

△ *Position the ball back in your stance to punch low shots (left), and forward to hit high shots. Play around with the loft, too.*

Devote a certain amount of your time to developing a series of 'comfort' zones with each of your pitching clubs. Then, thinking like a pro, you can make the most of these premium scoring shots, and calculate yardages with precision on the course.

The most effective way of gathering this information is to hit a number of full shots with each of your specialist wedges and measure off the average yardage in each specific case. This is not a test of how far you can hit each club, so don't swing wildly at the ball. The issue here is one of accuracy, so focus on controlling the speed of your swing with the rotation of your body, and try to group shots closely together.

Having discovered your range with a full swing, go to work on the in-between shots, the fiddly yardages that require you to manufacture a swing and gauge distance with awareness and feel. Set out a number of targets, and pitch balls between them at random. Find out what sort of swing you need to produce shots of 40, 50 and 60 yards. Switch clubs to discover how easily you can vary the trajectory of these 'part' shots.

Trial and error really is the most potent education. Don't be afraid to play around with your set-up position. If you want to hit a lower, running shot, play the ball back in your stance and make a conscious effort to swing a little more inside the line going back; if you want to hit a high, soft shot, move the ball forward in your stance, open the clubface at address and work on swinging across the ball from out to in.

Here's another drill that will test your feel and control. Set a marker at 10 yards, and stick an umbrella in the ground at a distance of around 50 yards. Then see how many balls you can stagger between the two markers, each successive shot flying farther than the one before it. As soon as a shot falls short of the previous one, the game's over. Set yourself performance targets, and see how you respond to a little pressure.

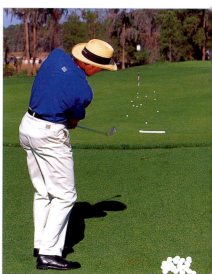

PITCHING: *Things to look out for*

BODY TOO SQUARE

From an open stance, good pitching technique involves a player turning his body back and forth to release the clubhead freely along the line to the hole. In contrast, the player who positions his body too squarely to that line (as with chipping) denies himself such freedom. He gets 'in his own way', and as a result must use his hands and arms to steer the ball forward. Remember, the quality of your swing is determined by the quality of your set-up position, and in order to create a repeating method it's vital that you set up with your lower body at least 20° or 30° open in relation to the target. In effect, you simply create your impact position at address – that's the key to a good set-up.

BACKSWING TOO LONG

Measuring the length of your swing to suit the length of the shot in question is a fundamental element in your short-game education. What you must avoid at all costs is making too long a backswing, and then decelerating the clubhead through impact in a last-ditch effort to control the distance you hit the ball. That simply does not wash. Instead, focus on developing the rotary motion of your body and controlling the distance you fly the ball with the speed of your swing.

SAND PLAY: *A simple case of mind over matter*

IN THE PROCESS OF sizing up an approach shot, pros don't view sand with the same trepidation as you probably do. As a matter of fact, most would rather wind up in a greenside bunker than leave the ball in the fringe grass, where the lie and the reaction of the ball can be uncertain. Why do they feel so confident? The obvious answer is that they spend many hours practicing their bunker skills, and feel quite at home in the sand. But more important than that, they understand why the sand iron is designed the way it is, and they know how to make good use of its special properties.

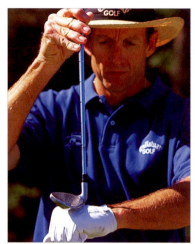

Let me take a moment to press home the importance of the sand iron, and the way its unique design can help you to develop confidence. Study the photograph on the right and you will notice that, as the club is positioned squarely, the heavy flange of the sole sits lower than the leading edge. This feature gives the club what we refer to as a 'bounce' effect. And the lower the back flange sits in relation to the leading edge, the greater is this measure of 'bounce'.

Now, look what happens as the clubface is turned open, as it would be to play a typical greenside sand shot. That degree of bounce effectively increases. So, depending on the way you set the club down and make your grip, you can control and adjust the amount of bounce present through impact, according to the lie of the ball, the texture of the sand and the nature of the shot you have to play.

This is the one shot in golf in which the objective is not to hit the ball, but rather the sand behind and beneath it. The art of a skillful bunker player is using this element of bounce to assist in skimming the clubhead through the sand beneath the ball. As you prepare to go away and practice, your job is to gauge the bounce required in a given situation, and deliver a shallow, glancing blow that cuts a swathe of sand, thus popping the ball into the air.

THE GRIP: The first thing to remember when preparing to play a regular greenside sand shot is to open the clubface before making your grip. Doing so eliminates the common mistake of taking a normal grip (with the clubface square), and then turning the hands to the right to open the clubface at address, which inevitably leads to the clubface closing and digging through impact. Adjusting the position of the clubface before completing your grip is fundamental to good bunker play – you simply turn the clubface a few degrees to the right, as you look at it, and then adopt your regular grip, with the loft and bounce pre-set.

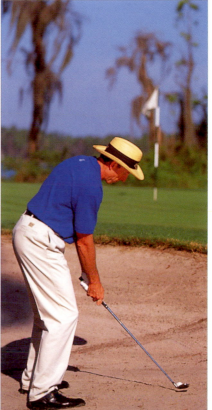

THE SET-UP: The mechanics of a regular bunker shot are straightforward. To compensate for the open clubface, you must stand with your body open in relation to the target line – somewhere between 30° and 45° open, depending on the distance you have to fly the ball. The shorter the shot, the more open the stance should be. Play the ball in the forward part of your stance, shuffle your shoes into the sand for a stable footing, flex your knees, and feel that your weight is evenly placed.

THE SWING: Once you have created that open stance, your body determines the line of your swing. Don't make the mistake of aiming left only to pick the club up too steeply outside the line of your body. Do that and you will lose the all-important connection between your arm-swing and body-turn, and deliver the club at too steep an angle.

So, aiming the clubface at a spot two to three inches behind the ball, swing the club back along the line of your body, and let your wrists hinge naturally to create a flowing rhythm. Swing the club smoothly through to the target, staying down on the shot, and splash the sand and the ball out onto the green.

Rhythm is a key factor, and a useful tip is to keep your feet flat in the sand as you accelerate toward the target and skim the open clubface beneath the ball. Make a fairly full swing and trust the fact that the sand will absorb the speed and energy of the clubhead. Distance is controlled in this case by the amount of acceleration through the shot, not by the length of the backswing. Control the distance you fly the ball with the length of your follow-through, but remember, you must always accelerate the clubhead beneath the sand through impact.

Memorise this five-point plan for your basic bunker technique:

1   *Open the clubface, then make your grip.*
2   *Aiming about 30° or so left of the target, shuffle your feet*
    into the sand for balance.
3   *Focus on a spot in the sand two to three inches behind the ball.*
4   *Swing the club back along your body line, stay down with it through*
    impact, and always accelerate through the shot.
5   *Control length of shot with length of follow-through.*

Follow these rules, trust the mechanics, and you will transform your sand game. Banish from your mind any ideas of lifting the ball out of the sand; your only consideration is that of accelerating the open clubface beneath the ball, using the sand as a buffer, which will create upward momentum.

SOUND ADVICE: *Thump, listen, and learn...*

Next time you go to practice, spend a few minutes in a bunker rehearsing your swing without a ball. Find a good, level lie and play at 'thumping' the sand. Try to get that open clubface bouncing through at various speeds, each delivery removing a nice, shallow divot. Draw a line in the sand and practice hitting that line on a regular basis to enhance your control of the clubhead through impact. Think in terms of throwing a divot of sand toward the hole, and listen to the sound you make.

Pretty soon you will distinguish good shot from bad by the sound you make as you hit the sand. A promising 'thwack' will achieve much better results than a dull 'thud'. A dynamic sound signals that the open clubface is entering and exiting the sand correctly; the flange is making first contact, and the 'bounce' is working as it should.

Make a few swings with your eyes closed, too. That will further heighten your awareness of good technique, and help you to develop a nice, consistent rhythm. After a few minutes, put a line of balls in the sand and make the same swings same sound, same feel.

I like to think in terms of controlling the length of the follow-through. Work on repeating a fairly long backswing for all shots – that sets a consistent rhythm – and if you want to hit the ball farther, aim to increase the length of the follow-through. That also increases your acceleration. Don't make the common mistake of swinging too short, and then stabbing the sand.

With this technique, and variations on it, you can and should practice from every conceivable situation in a bunker. Vary the lie of the ball, running from a perfectly clean lie to an ugly, buried one. Work on hitting the ball high, on getting it to climb quickly to avoid the front lip, and zip the clubhead through the sand to create backspin. These are all merely variations on a basic theme – opening the clubface, using the bounce, and slicing sand from beneath the ball.

You might not go to the extremes of Gary Player, one of the world's finest ever bunker players, who would stay in the bunker until he had holed five shots, but a little work along these lines will go a long way toward building confidence.

SPLASH OFF A BOARD: *Learn technique, gain confidence*

For many players, trusting the bounce of the clubhead to remove a divot of sand, and the ball, is something that takes time, but this drill can help you overcome that anxiety, and very quickly rewards you with the sensation of a well-executed splash shot.

Take a short board, or plank of wood, and bury it in the sand as I have done here. Cover the board with at least an inch of sand, place a ball on top, and prepare for action. Using your sand iron, set yourself up to play a regular splash shot, and simply bounce the clubhead on the board, removing a nice cut of sand – and the ball – in one smooth motion. Don't be afraid of it: make a nice, free-flowing swing, and splash the sand off the board as the club bounces through.

After a few minutes, remove the board but go after the same swing and impact sensations with the ball sitting normally. Remember, open the clubface before completing your grip, and accelerate through the sand.

SPECIALITY SHOT: *The secret of 'delicate aggression'*

Here's a problem you will often face: your ball is lying well in a bunker, but the pin is cut just a few yards away, and the lip is severe. What you need is a shot that climbs steeply and stops quickly. You must accelerate the clubhead through the sand, but you don't want the ball to go too far. Let me demonstrate a professional solution – a shot for the better player.

First, set your body alignment more open than normal. Set up at least 45° open to the target, and play the ball forward in your stance, opposite your left instep. Make sure your hands are behind the ball. Then, having severely opened the clubface, weaken your right-hand grip. Make sure the right hand is well on top of the left as you look down. This final adjustment will help you to keep the clubface open through the shot, and enables you to be aggressive through the sand.

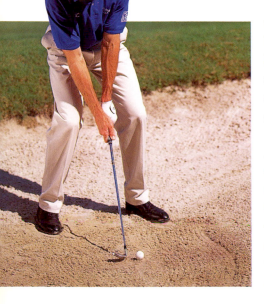

Once you are comfortable over the ball, think about the rhythm of your swing. Make a fairly full but lazy backswing, and then control your acceleration with the length of your follow-through, in this case a fairly short, stabby, affair. The open clubface removes a shallow cut of sand, and the ball floats out, flying as if in slow motion, and settles down quickly.

Maintaining that open clubface is the key to success here, and when you practice this shot your thoughts should be of cupping your left wrist and rotating the clubface as you swing the club away from the ball, so that you expose the maximum loft possible. Another thought to have is that of the right hand working under the left through impact, which further protects that open clubface and guarantees a shallow divot of sand. As you finish your swing and hold your follow-through, the clubface should be looking straight up at the sky.

PLAY DRAW-BACK FOR FEEL... *and fine-tune your touch*

The American Ryder Cup player Brad Faxon, a fine sand player, works on a great drill that helps him to fine-tune distance control out of a greenside bunker. He takes a bucket of balls, aims to land the first one as close to the hole as possible, and then with each subsequent ball plays 'draw-back', trying to get each ball closer to the lip of the bunker. As soon as he lands a ball beyond the previous shot, the game's over.

      This type of exercise quickly teaches you to associate the speed of your swing and the nature of impact with the distance a ball flies and the way it reacts on the green. Your focus must be on accelerating the club through the sand, and controlling distance with the length of your through-swing. Before too long you will begin to associate the length of your swing with a particular length of shot, which will develop your feel for control.

SPECIALITY SHOT: *V-shape swing deals with plugged ball*

If you can imagine a rounded, U-shape swing taking care of the majority of the bunker shots you are likely to come across, then a slightly steeper, V-shaped action is your weapon when the ball is plugged. That enables you to dig beneath the bottom of the ball, and get to the root of the problem, so to speak.

For a partially plugged ball, such as the example you see here, I would suggest you use your sand iron, or possibly a wedge, but with the clubface this time square to the line of the shot. You want the club to dig down into the sand (not bounce through it) so, as you take up your regular grip, make sure the leading edge is square to the line of the target. Square up your stance, too, and, with the majority of your weight on your left side, play the ball in the middle of your feet.

The swing itself should be a straightforward 'up-and-down' affair, though it must be executed with commitment. Pick the club up with a sharp wrist break (thus creating that steepness in your swing), and then thump the sand fairly close to the ball. There will be little or no follow-through – as you bury the clubhead, you literally blast the ball out with a controlled explosion. Because of the amount of sand that has to be taken, allow for a little more overspin and roll than normal.

When you face a shot where the sand is unusually hard or wet, consider using a wedge, which has less bounce. The sharper leading edge will assist you in digging beneath the ball – just be aggressive, stay down on the shot, and allow for a lot of run.

SAND PLAY: *Things to look out for*

BACKSWING TOO SHORT

In order to create the momentum sufficient to displace both sand and ball, good bunker technique requires a fairly full and flowing swing. The speed of the delivery determines the distance of the shot, but a good player will exhibit tremendous 'flow' in his method. In contrast, a fault that troubles many amateur players is that of making too short a backswing, followed by what can best be described as a flinch at the ball. There is little in the way of rhythm, and the clubhead disappears into the sand.

The point I will stress here is that you must not be afraid to make a fairly full and fluent swing. Don't worry about hitting the ball too far, as the sand absorbs the energy of your swing – as long as you hit it before the ball!

Remember, as long as you open the clubface before you make your grip – and keep it open throughout your swing – you can be aggressive, and yet the ball will only travel a short distance...trust me!

STRAIGHT LEGS IN DOWNSWING

A tendency to 'stand up' and straighten the legs during the downswing is another symptom of anxiety, and signals to me that a player is not fully at ease with the basic technique. Again, it's a matter of trust. Just as they do in the full swing, the knees play a critical role in stabilizing the upper body as you turn back and through. So, having flexed your knees nicely at address, it's important that you maintain that flex up to the point of impact in order to maintain your levels and control the amount of sand you take.

PRACTICING TO PLAY

I AM OFTEN ASKED what separates the winners from the 'also-rans' on the pro tours around the world, and invited to assess the potential of many aspiring golfers who visit my base in Orlando, Florida, and my other Academy sites around the world. And while technical ability ranks high in any appraisal I make, far more important to me is a player's attitude, his style of thinking, his commitment to the game and his desire to succeed. Look up and down the practice tee at any tournament these days and it would appear that any one of a hundred talented players has the game to win. They all seem to strike the ball imperiously, and look every inch a champion. But only a few ever make it to the very top. There is a certain character that distinguishes a winner, a strength of mind and self-discipline that encapsulates the attributes above and makes all the difference.

The same is true in amateur golf. No matter what the standard of play, or the handicaps involved, it is the player who displays this affinity for *playing the game* who comes out on top. This is the golfer who prepares himself for the challenge; who thinks strategically on the course; and who is prepared to take the rough with the smooth. If you like, the player who can turn theory into practice.

ABOUT 'TRAINING' AND 'TRUSTING'

Here's the real problem: *practicing* and *playing* golf are two very different things. Think about it for a moment. On the practice tee you have the luxury of a perfectly level lie every time you set up to make a swing. The ball sits cleanly. There are no hazards to threaten your composure, no water to avoid and no penalties for hitting a poor shot. And if you do hit a bad one, you forget about it, and pull another one from the pile. Of course, you have certain goals and expectations as regards the overall quality of your ball-striking, but without a card and pencil in your hand, or an opponent to intimidate you, you can enjoy hitting shots one after another, and soon get into a comfortable, stress-free routine.

Contrast that situation with the reality of the game. A golf course is a living challenge, and your ability to maintain focus and concentration over 18 holes is pulled this way and that. When you go out to play you will experience all sorts of changing conditions; a course rarely plays the same way twice. One day the wind can blow from the north, the next it comes from the south. You create a good, level lie on the tee, but after that it's pretty much a lottery. No matter how well you might be striking the ball, the bounce is utterly unpredictable, and you need your wits about you to deal with the uneven lies and other demanding ground conditions the game has in store. You are now also confronted with hazards, out-of-bounds and so on – none of which exist on the practice tee, but all of which tries your patience and tests your character as a golfer.

If I might borrow a phrase from the well-known sports psychologist, Dr. Bob Rotella, a successful player is one who recognizes up front that 'golf is not a game of perfect'. If practicing golf is a test of your physical ability, then playing the game determines the quality of that preparation and examines your mental toughness and ability to replicate skills under pressure. That pressure comes in many forms. It may come from your playing partners – the pressure of not losing a match, or failing in front of your peers. It may come from the pressure of a big-day tournament, after working so hard toward a certain fixture you want to do well and impress your friends. A great deal of stress can be self-inflicted and the result of your own high expectations, which can breed a certain type of negative thinking. For example. you might say to yourself: 'Three pars to finish and I will shoot my best score'. This is negative because you can't control two shots from now, let alone think three holes down the road. Thus the importance of staying 'in the present', as we will discuss in a moment.

In the sterile environment of the practice tee these issues are of no consequence, but out on the golf course they are very real, and unless you learn to think straight and focus on playing one shot at a time, they threaten to cloud your judgement and inhibit your performance. To survive, and make that transition from training your physical skills to trusting them when it matters most, your creativity and strength of mind – like your golf swing – must be worked on and developed.

In a nutshell, you have to learn to practice to play. To bridge the mental gap that exists between the 'practice mode' and the 'playing mode' you must introduce a degree of realism into your strategy that enables you to experience certain 'playing mode' pressures on the practice tee, and program your mind effectively so that you respond positively to challenges out on the course. That might involve something as simple as varying your location on the practice tee at regular intervals to avoid getting 'stale', learning to play shots from all sorts of difficult lies, or simply working through clubs at random, and fine-tuning your pre-shot routine. These and a number of other related techniques illustrated in this chapter serve one common purpose: they keep your mind alert. Many of the ideas have proved successful with the tour players I work with, and my hope is that you will incorporate these same exercises into your own practice schedule so that you develop your capacity for playing the game.

POSITIVE MIND GAMES

WHY DO TOUR PLAYERS work so hard on repeating good habits in practice? Simple. They work hard behind the scenes because they don't want to be thinking about complicated 'mechanics' when they walk up to the last hole of a tournament with a narrow lead and a 4-iron shot over water to a slim green. That's when they switch to auto-pilot – just the way they practiced it. I touched on the importance of the pre-shot routine in the opening chapter, and many references have been made to it since, but it's worth reinforcing the point. A good swing is an instinctive reaction, a habit you foster with hours of work on the practice tee. A cast-iron pre-shot routine is the most basic and effective tool at your disposal for accessing a good swing out on the course, where it matters most. In reality, the shot starts from the time you walk up to the ball.

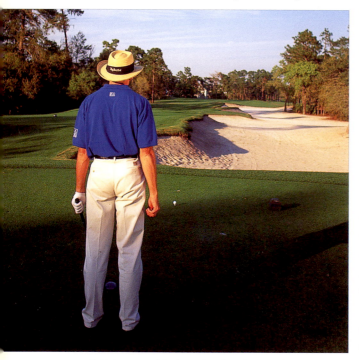

△ *Take a good look at the shot that confronts you. Pick out your target and visualize the shape you want to play.*

A good routine is a natural routine and while every player has his or her own preferences for detail, it must be thoroughly consistent. It's no good taking 10 seconds on one shot, and 40 seconds on the next. Such erratic behavior reflects uncertainty, or a lack of focus, and so is unlikely to yield a repeating swing. Similarly, I don't like to see a student of mine waggle the club four times with the driver, and then just once with the 5-iron. A repeating swing demands a repeating routine. Right through the bag, up to the little shots around the green, where it could vary from a full shot, it is this element of routine that enables you to stay focused on the shot at hand and relaxed over the ball. You can expect minor variations in your routine over the course of a round – that is human nature. However, any significant changes, such as those mentioned above, generally spell trouble.

Strictly speaking, the pre-shot routine begins the moment you pick a club out of the bag, though of course by that time your senses will have informed you of a number of other relevant factors that need to be taken care of. First, you have to assess a situation thoroughly, taking into account the distance to the target, the quality of the lie and the strength and direction of any wind that might affect the flight of the ball. Once this data has been fed into the computer, you can make a strategic decision and select the appropriate club.

Make a pact with yourself that you will never set up to the ball with doubt in your mind over club selection. Indecision in club selection almost always leads to poor execution.

Having made this appraisal, the final countdown begins with a last 'absorbing' look at the target. Ideally, you want to get into the habit of standing directly behind the ball, so that you can visualize the shot and see it working out just the way you planned it. Just like the high-jumper who focuses on the height of the bar and pictures himself leaping over it, your thoughts must be geared to success.

It is at this point that you must pick a target at which to hit the ball. For example, with the driver (or any full tee shot), get into the habit of picking a target above ground level, such as the top of a tree or a distant chimney. Hitting at some distinct landmark is much less threatening, psychologically, than trying to split the fairway. Just make sure the target you choose allows for your natural ball-flight tendency (i.e. draw or fade). Also, make the target as small and specific as possible. You should be able to describe it in detail if asked. A small target gives you less room for error and your body will respond to it with practice.

The majority of players I work with take this a stage further, and pick out an intermediate target (perhaps an old divot mark or piece of dirt) just in front of the ball, which helps them to take aim. Jack Nicklaus has used this technique throughout his career, and if you watch him you will notice that he looks up at this intermediate target several times before pulling the trigger and setting his swing in motion. His reasoning is simple: it's much easier to focus on a target a few feet in front of the ball than it is on the flag far away in the distance. Another thought to ponder...

Once you have that clear picture logged in your mind, approach the ball in a slight semi-circle, and position yourself in such a way that your body is square to the target line as you place the club behind the ball, all the time conscious of that intermediate target. When you are satisfied that the clubface is aimed correctly, complete your grip and stance. Some players like to stand with their feet together, the and ball dead center, and then adjust the position of their left foot to determine the ball position, and the position of their right foot

▽ *Keep the image of your target in your mind as you walk in to assume your position over the ball.*

to establish the desired width of stance. Others like to place their right foot forward while aligning the clubface, and then bring the left foot into place. But however you choose to run through the set-up routine, make sure it is consistent, and that on a full shot your feet, knees, hips and shoulders are parallel with the ball-to-target line. Once you feel you are aligned correctly, you can really get into the act of visualizing and sensing the shot, using your intermediate target as a spot you want to get the ball started over on its flight to the target. Finally, incorporating a waggle – or some form of motion at the start – is the way to get your engine revved and ready for action.

That waggle is important. It serves to rid your hands and arms of any lingering tension, and also helps you to get a clear mental picture of the moveaway and the path the club should follow in the first few feet of the swing, which are critical. It also gives you a greater sense of feel for the type of shot you are about to play – a fade, a draw. I personally like players to waggle the club a couple of times while looking at the target, and then, once the eyes have refocused on the ball, to consider some sort of final pressure release – a slight forward press, a kink of the right knee or a slight turning of the head – to set the wheels smoothly in motion.

Think of all the great players who have made some particular habit or other their trademark – players such as Gary Player (with the gentle kicking-in of the right knee), Jack Nicklaus (with his turning away of the head at the start of the swing) and Nick Faldo (hitching the trousers and two brisk waggles) prove the value of good habits. Tom Watson is another good waggler of the club. The key is to develop a natural looking motion to

▽ *Carefully aim the clubface at your target and then complete your routine, aligning your feet, hips and shoulders parallel with the target line.*

preempt the swing, that prevents tension creeping in, and gets the swing off to a smooth rhythmical start.

These distinct personal rituals are not exclusive to golf. Tennis legend Ivan Lendl would bounce the ball seven times before hitting a serve. That was his pre-shot routine. Those seven bounces enabled him to get focused; they created repetition, a sense of 'been here before', and that's the key. Similarly, goal-kickers follow a set pattern of steps before the run up to the ball; in basketball, players have their own very individual habits before taking a free-throw, bouncing the ball a set number of times to calm the nerves and ready themselves to replicate a skill they have trained for a thousand times in practice.

It's up to you to nurture your own trademark. And once you have a set routine, practicing it is just as important as practicing your swing. Think about it between balls; stand back a moment to stop and think about the type of shot you want to hit; give your mind something positive to focus on, and go through the steps of your routine.

It all boils down to standardizing behavior. A disciplined pre-shot routine will help you to combat pressure and repeat skills you have learned in practice. Ultimately, you want to spend a consistent amount of time on each shot, and hone certain personal traits that enable you to relax over the ball and repeat a nice easy swinging motion. And remember, if anything should interrupt your routine or disturb your train of thought as you prepare to play a shot, walk away and start over again. The extra care and attention you give will lead to you hitting better shots and thus fewer strokes and less time overall.

▽ *Waggle the clubhead, and get ready to make your swing.*

'SEE' THE COURSE, AND PLAY IT: *Positive images, positive thoughts*

Hitting balls one after another with the same club is acceptable practice behavior when you are working on some particular element of your technique, but it doesn't begin to equate with playing the game. How can it? Beating balls from the same level lie with the same club is good for developing your muscle memory, but it does not challenge your imagination or gear your mind and body toward hitting a target – which is exactly what you must do on the course.

One of the most effective exercises I know for developing 'playing' skills on the practice tee is the mental rehearsal drill we touched upon briefly in Chapter 1 – 'seeing' a specific shot, and playing it. This involves visualizing holes and putting yourself in a realistic situation on a particular hole, and it is worth building on this concept as a means of making this transition between practicing 'swing' and playing golf.

With the help of a yardage chart – and a lively imagination – you can play a complete round of golf without leaving the practice tee, and in the process rehearse all of the shots you know you will need out on the course for real. It works like this. Imagine you are standing on the 1st tee at your home club (see illustration below). Take whatever club you would expect to use, run through your pre-shot routine, visualize the shot you would like to hit, and put the ball in play. Watch the ball in the air and use your imagination to gauge where it would have finished on that particular hole. Figure out the approximate yardage you would have left to the green, and play your second shot. And so the game goes on.

If you take this exercise seriously, and give due consideration to each shot, it can take you up to 30 minutes to play an imaginary 18 holes, excluding the short game, and at the end of that time your mind will be fully in-tune with the course. Rather than just beating balls for half an hour, this mental rehearsal technique is an extremely effective means of warming up for a game, and I strongly recommend it, particularly to students who are prone to getting too technical in their thinking. I would advise players to wind up their regular warm-up session by playing at least the first three or four holes prior to the 1st tee. This should help to get you off to a good start, which is important.

▷ *Practicing to music helps certain players fine-tune their tempo – particularly in the short game.*

Visualizing a realistic situation and applying yourself to it can also help you to deal with pressure and overcome any mental blocks you might have about playing a particular hole, or hitting a certain club. Let's say you live in fear of hooking out of bounds at the short 14th, where a fence runs the entire left-hand side of the fairway. 'Seeing' that hole on the practice tee, and playing the tee-shot over and over again in your mind, can help you to beat that fear of failure, and emerge a stronger player.

Remember, the more often you put yourself under a pressure situation in practice – such as facing a tee shot with out-of-bounds left, hitting a long iron to a par-3 over water, or holing a left-to-right breaking four-footer to win the club championship – the better equipped you will be to deal with this pressure when it hits you for real on the course. It's a means of cleansing the communication lines between your brain and body.

You can expand upon this concept at home. Johnny Miller used to say that, sitting alone on the eve of a tournament, he would close his eyes and dream about great rounds he had played, sensing the atmosphere of success. This would help him find a 'winning' state of mind. It created all the right positive feelings that he needed to go out and produce his best golf. Anything you can do to give yourself the sense of having experienced a situation before can benefit your game… reading books on golf and watching videos of great players in action can motivate you to raise the level of your own performance… dreaming about a 'personal best' score as you go to sleep the night before a tournament can help to prepare you for success. All of these activities leave bold, positive images in your mind.

To take another angle, I have had many students who improve their practice sessions tremendously by practicing to music. They say listening to relaxing music through earphones helps them to find and repeat their true rhythm, and gets them focused on swinging the clubhead. Some prefer to hum or whistle a tune. Fuzzy Zoeller and Mark McCumber whistle and hum their way round a golf course as a means of relieving pressure, to maintain their rhythm between shots and so stay relaxed.

A number of tour players in America use a metronome (which you can purchase inexpensively from any music store) when they practice, particularly on the putting green. It helps them to find and then repeat their personal rhythm. Fast or slow – it doesn't matter. The important thing is that you repeat a consistent tempo on every stroke, and the metronome teaches you this control. Your internal rhythm is most likely to change under pressure. Your tendency may be to rush, to swing too quickly, or to slow down and take four practice swings rather than two. So anything you can do in practice to instil this sense of monotonous 'one-two' consistency is good for your game. Don't knock it til' you've tried it!

HOW TO STAY RELAXED: *Focus on breathing pattern*

Every player has his own scoring threshold – be it to break 100, 90, 80 or 70. We feel comfortable whenever a round is ticking along as normal, when we are headed for another score that pretty much reflects our handicap and what others expect of us. But what happens when you find yourself in line to shoot an all-time low number? Suddenly, it feels uncomfortable. Now you are in unchartered territory, out of your 'comfort zone', and you begin to doubt your ability to finish the job. With perhaps four or five holes to play you lose the 'present tense' focus and positive frame of mind that enabled you to get into this position, and as the pressure builds your anxiety gets in the way of your score.

To play well and sustain your game over the course of 18 holes, it is vital that you remain relaxed. If you begin to feel 'tight', or anxious, there is a danger you might speed up between shots, walk a little more briskly than normal, and hurry your pre-shot routine. These are typical symptoms of the pressure we associate with breaking through a personal 'comfort zone', and it's important that you are able to recognize these tendencies, so that you can do something about it.

One of the easiest and most effective ways of controlling your rhythm and tempo out on the course is through your breathing pattern. We touched on this in Chapter 1, where I suggested that a controlled breathing pattern can help you to beat 1st-tee nerves, and indeed that principle can be applied to any stressful situation. When you find yourself under pressure, a number of things happen. The smaller muscles in your body begin to tighten, your heart rate increases, your body becomes tense and might feel awkward, and you begin to think too hard about what it is you are trying to do. Slowly but surely these reactions undermine the fluidity of your swing and your presence of mind, but a controlled series of deep-breathing exercises can alleviate the tension.

Try this on the practice tee. Address a ball, and take a nice, deep breath as you waggle the club. Then exhale throughout the whole swing. Start breathing out the moment you start your backswing and keep it going until you complete your follow-through. Pace your swing with that smooth exhalation of air. Concentrate on nothing other than breathing deeply in and out, and hit a few shots.

This technique works with every club in the bag – especially on and around the green – and is a real defence mechanism in the face of mounting pressure. Breaking through your comfort zone is tough, but this breathing exercise can help to take your mind off your score, and will leave your body relaxed enough to make a good swing. The key is to focus on playing one shot at a time.

Deep breathing is also a valuable means of relaxing as you walk between shots. I work with players who tell me that, over the closing holes of a tournament, they think about nothing else but breathing deeply as they walk from tee to green, so they feel in control of their mind *and* body when they arrive at their ball.

Your posture and body language also reveals a great deal about your mental state. Players who tend to slouch their shoulders and walk with their head low have usually thrown in the towel; those who stand tall and walk with purpose are more positive, and mean business right up to the final putt. Their body language reflects how they want to feel. Even on the practice tee, when things are not going well, maintain your poise and remember that good golf is as much about good attitude as good swings.

GAMES YOU SHOULD PLAY: *Test imagination, create pressure*

To supplement your work on the range, and other mental rehearsal exercises you might use at home, make the most of any opportunity you have to practice out on the course, where you can create 'real' situations and test both your physical and mental skills. There are a number of games you can play, one of the easiest being to pit one ball against another, odd number versus even, so that you create a matchplay-type situation. Again, you introduce an element of pressure, which hardens your ability to repeat a good swing. Better players might take this a stage further, and play a draw against a fade, or nominate specific shots in different situations to test their ability to work the ball.

Another way to practice competitively on your own terms is to play what I call 'two-ball-worst-ball'. You simply play two balls from the tee, and then play another two balls from wherever the worse shot finishes, and so on until you finish the hole, and note down your score. Alternatively, restrict yourself to hitting no more than a 5-iron off the tee on the par-4's and 5's. This is a particularly worthwhile exercise for those players who tend to spend most of their time on a fairly short course, as it demands that you hit the longer irons and woods for your approach shots to the green, where normally you pull out a 9-iron or wedge.

On another day you might consider carrying just three or four clubs, one of them being a putter, and see how you score over 9 holes. This is a real test of your imagination and versatility; when you don't have the exact club for a certain yardage, you have to invent and manufacture shots, which is a skill in itself and one that every golfer must develop. You might be surprised at the results. A good number of '3-club' competitions are won with scores lower than those posted in normal events, because (1) players are not tempted by the driver, and so tend to keep the ball in play, and (2) they are forced to think a little harder about distances and landing areas on their shots to the green – i.e. there is a greater awareness of strategy and course management.

The lesson to be learned here is that good scoring on the course can be accomplished in a variety of ways, and a further benefit of this exercise is that it will instil in you the confidence to keep a score going, even though you might not be swinging well.

The issue of distance control is a significant factor in your education as a golfer, and taking 'a little off' your iron shots, hitting 'knock-down' shots and 'bunting the ball' will teach you real control. Consider all of these shots on the practice tee. To work on his control, Sam Snead used to practice hitting the same distance shot with five different clubs. Say he normally hit a 7-iron 150 yards, he would then try to hit the 6, 5, 4 and 3-iron to the 150-yard marker, all the while maintaining a good flight and trajectory. This is a better player's exercise, and is a lot tougher than you might think.

Remember, iron clubs are not distance clubs. They are all about accuracy. Swing too hard and not only will you be prone to mis-hitting the ball, but your ability to control landing distances will be erratic. As an exercise, make yourself 'club-up' on every approach shot next time you play a few practice holes on the course – i.e. take a 7-iron where normally you would hit an 8-iron. I'd be surprised if you not only strike the ball better than normal, but also straighter and nearer the hole. Don't be satisfied with finishing on the front of the green – get the ball to at least pin-height. Generally speaking, it would be true to say that playing within yourself is a quality you need to develop if you want to hit consistently solid shots.

SHORT-GAME SKILLS CHALLENGE:
Make the most of competitive practice

Competition sharpens your mind and adds a valuable dimension to your practice time. The short game, in particular, offers tremendous scope for imagination, and you should make the most of any opportunity to invent challenges – preferably against a player of similar or slightly superior ability. There is so much scope on and around a green. Invent a matchplay situation – test each other on chipping, pitching, and bunker play. Hit three balls each from the same location, and see who can get up and down most often. Alternatively, scatter a handful of balls around a green, and then challenge each other to get up and down from wherever they come to rest. Have fun. Set targets, and try to beat them. Invent putting competitions to test each other under pressure – particularly on critical four-footers that win and lose matches. Wager a small bet.

These games take your mind off 'technique', make you focus on the target, and help you to develop your immunity to pressure. The more you indulge in this type of realistic practice, the faster you will improve your performance and your capacity for lower scoring.

A game I like to play on the putting green with a sparring partner is to take two holes 20 or 30 feet apart and, with each player standing next to the hole, putt to the opposite one, as you see here with US tour player, Tom Shearer. As soon as a putt is holed, swap ends. Play the first to reach 5 or 10 points. It helps you groove a stroke, while at the same time competing.

PRACTICE SCHEDULES: *Make the most of your time*

In my experience, most players fail to utilize their practice time as effectively as they could. It's the same old story: the driving-range is full, but the short-game area is deserted. Time is precious to us all, but organizing what time you do have available to work on your game will make practice more effective.

When I discuss time-management with students I draw their attention to three distinct phases of practice, and it's worth considering these to identify your own position within an overall program of development. First, there is the **'building and development'** one, which includes beginners taking lessons to learn the fundamentals and more seasoned players who choose to go back to basics in search of a better game (as Nick Faldo did when he decided to remodel his swing in 1985). The second phase is a **'refining'** phase, during which a player fine-tunes his or her swing changes, working on drills to make new moves more natural. Third is the **'maintenance'** phase – the ultimate state to be in. Happy with the way you are playing, your chief concern here is on improving scoring skills out on the course.

Ideally, we would all like to be in the maintenance phase, but to achieve such a level of proficiency you have to spend time in the earlier phases, in sequence. And even players who reach phase three will, at times, find it necessary to go back to phase two (in Nick's case to phase one) to improve their game and stay on top of their form.

Identifying your phase of learning is important, in my opinion, because it determines your mode of learning. In the development stage I would expect a player to work on a number of drills, to be fairly relaxed about the outcome of each shot, and to focus his attention on details of technique rather than concerning himself with the target. To emphasize that point I advise pupils to hit balls in groups of six at a time, and in this phase recommend a technique-to-target thought ratio of 6:0 (in the building stage, your thoughts should revolve purely around technique).

Working more on static positions, I would also expect there to be a certain amount of video analysis, checking certain points in swing, and the practice schedule would reflect that. In this phase of development a player should not worry about scoring or get upset about hitting poor shots – that all comes with the territory!

The big danger is never getting out of phase one, but mapping out an effective schedule will help you to reach phase two, the refinement stage, where you work on slight changes to improve your ball-striking – tinkering here and there, hitting some good shots, but lacking consistency. In this phase, practice is a blend of technique and target, working on drills that improve rhythm and motion, and thinking in terms of the full swing rather than pieces. In terms of those six balls, I would suggest in this case that a player work on a ratio of 4:2 – i.e. hit four balls while focusing on your technique, and two while thinking about the target.

In the maintenance phase, a player is happy with his overall game, and playing well. Practice sessions are heavily weighted in favor of the short game, with the emphasis on sharpening scoring skills. The ratio of technique-to-target is now 0:6 – i.e. all conscious thought is directed toward finding the target. To stay sharp, I further encourage players who reach this level to work on varying their position around a green and to hit all sorts of shots on the practice tee for a complete 14-club workout.

Wherever you stand in your development as a golfer, the key to designing an effective practice schedule is knowing that quality always beats quantity. You hear stories of players beating hundreds of balls, and certainly a fit, low-handicap player who enjoys hitting balls can practice in such a manner. I am not convinced, however, that this is the way to go. I think practicing within certain time schedules, focusing on what has to be done and hitting the necessary shots to obtain feedback, is more important.

I have often seen players who have practiced so hard that they have over-cooked what they are working on and as a result have got worse over time. One example comes to mind of a former business executive who was a respectable 8 handicap playing and practicing once a week. Upon retiring, he started to play and practice five times a week. In three months his handicap went up to 12. Obviously in this case he was practicing the wrong things – so beware. The smart player will get more out of a good 1-hour session than many golfers will in a week on the range.

Let me give you two examples of the type of practice schedule I like my students to work on, with either a one- or two-hour time frame. I believe you should design your practice sessions to suit whatever time you have available, and deal with specific elements of the game that most need attention. Ideally, I would suggest that you set aside a two-hour window – one hour for the long game, one hour for the short game. If you have the

SCHEDULE A
Follow this two-hour session at least once a week.

THE LONG GAME

1. **The Warm-up:** Loosen-up your golfing muscles with basic stretching exercises, including the pivot-drill, swinging two clubs together, or swishing a club through long grass (*5 minutes*).

2. **Technical Session:** I recommend that you use a 5- or 6-iron when working on specific elements of the full swing (lay a club on the ground to confirm good alignment). For every ball, rehearse at least two drills or practice swings. Maximum number of balls – 40 (*30 minutes*). Then spend the remaining time working on clubs you seem to have a problem with – i.e. long iron, driver (*5 minutes*).

3. **Mental Rehearsal:** Adhering to your pre-shot routine, hit shots as if you were out on the course, 'seeing' the situation before selecting the appropriate club and putting the ball in play. Also, switch between clubs at random, and test yourself from a number of different and difficult lies (*15 minutes*).

4. **Winding Down:** Finish your session with a handful of wedge shots, pitching balls to random targets. Think about maintaining your rhythm and feel for the clubhead (*5 minutes*).

THE SHORT GAME

1. **The Warm-up:** Hit a few chip-shots and pitch-shots to get a little feel going. Try to group balls closely together, and switch between clubs to vary the height and trajectory of shots (*10 minutes*).

2. **Focus on Technique:** Based on your knowledge of your game, take a specific short-game skill (i.e. chipping, pitching or bunker play) and work on improving the technical elements of your method (*20 minutes*).

3. **Mental Rehearsal:** Create a real situation, and apply yourself to a particular shot as if you are playing for real on the course – that could be a chip, a pitch or a sand shot. Set performance targets and note the results (*15 minutes*).

4. **Putting:** Every short-game session should feature a spell of putting practice. Refer to recent performances to determine which elements of your putting most need attention. Work on drills to sharpen your stroke from short range, and to improve your sense of feel on the longer approach putts (*15 minutes*).

SCHEDULE B
If you have only one hour to practice, split your time as follows:

1. **The Warm-up:** Use basic stretching exercises to loosen up your golfing muscles as you prepare to work on your swing, and hit a handful of wedge shots to alert feel (*5 minutes*).

2. **Full-swing Technique:** Starting with a mid-iron, work on general ball-striking skills and focus particularly on rhythm and tempo. Work up to the longer clubs, and for every five shots, make sure two are executed with a full routine – i.e. focusing on the 'where' rather than the 'how' (*25 minutes*).

3. **See the course, and play it:** Play three holes you are familiar with at your golf course to get really focused on targets and routine (*5 minutes*).

4. **Short-game Spotlight:** Based on current performances, take one aspect of the short game and apply yourself to improving technique, using drills and practice games as necessary (*15 minutes*).

5. **Putting Practice:** Finish your one-hour session on the putting green, working on both the accuracy of your stroke from short range and your touch on lag putts (*10 minutes*).

opportunity to do more, set aside some time to go out and play a few holes alone, so that you can practice playing on the course.

It's a good idea to keep a diary of your practice sessions, too. Make a note of whatever it is you are working on. What particular swing thoughts seem to work best? Which drill gave you the feel that you needed to make a change? Over time, these notes will become extremely valuable to you, and will help you to keep your game in tip-top condition.

These are merely suggestions, and you must spend a few minutes designing your own plan, one that suits your needs and requirements at that particular time. For example, if you are happy with your long game, you might spend as little as ten minutes hitting full shots before heading to the short-game area. Practice your weaknesses, not your strengths – a point that I hope reinforces the importance of the self-analysis techniques we discussed in the opening chapter.

Realize also that a great deal of good can be achieved at home, where you are not inhibited by the prospect of hitting a ball. Swing with your eyes closed, make slow-motion swings, train with a weighted club, and check key swing positions in a mirror. This type of practice is especially helpful when you are working on changing technique and need to keep in touch with your swing feelings on a regular basis.

JUNIORS: *Enjoy the game, have fun*

I meet and advise many parents who are keen on their children playing golf. Some try to force the game on to their children, which is a mistake. A child must want to play for fun. Nothing else matters. Let them loose to hit balls from any age. Have an old 4- or 5-wood cut down, and let them play. Our two-year-old son has a small plastic club and loves trying to hit a plastic ball around the house. You're never too young to start!

I find that juniors tend to practice most effectively in short bursts – 20 minutes on swing theory at the most – and when I coach young players I keep details on technique to an absolute minimum. The basics of grip and set-up are important, naturally, and you should keep an eye on these elements of technique as they grow. But they don't need complicated theory. Instead, encourage them to watch other good players hit shots. Children imitate so well. They recognize good motion, and copy it.

The shape of a child's swing will change as he or she gets bigger and stronger, but touch and feel stay with a player for life. Which is why it is so important that you encourage them to participate in the short game. Invent competitions. Let them play with friends. A bucket of balls, a practice green and a bunker are all you need to set a young player on his way to becoming a skilled player and enjoying this great game. Let them experience ball-control from short range, and they will develop the hand-eye coordination common to every repeating swing. It's an enjoyable way to spend time with your children, so make their practice sessions fun and enjoyable, and let them go at their own pace.

▽ *The Leadbetter clan (l-r) James, Hally and Andy. ▷ Only when a junior reaches the age of 11 or 12 should practice become a little more specific – and then only if they are serious about playing golf. That's when you should seek out a good teaching pro who can take over their education and nurture their talent.*

TOOLS OF THE TRADE: *Accelerate the learning experience*

To give a player a heightened sense of feel and enforce good practice habits, I have designed and endorsed a number of training aids over the last five or ten years. They range from simple instruments of learning, such as a mirror that can be positioned around you as you practice, to a swing trainer that helps you to build and develop the muscles you need for good golf. These products, and others that I use in my teaching, assist me in communicating that highly elusive quality we call *feel*. When you practice, never lose sight of the fact that feeling mechanics and repeating them is much easier to sustain than purely thinking about them. Many of the tour players I coach have used these products in their practice sessions. In this game, I have found that anything that can give you an edge to achieve your goals is worth experimenting with. Practicing really is a game within a game: it is at the same time rewarding and fulfilling, challenging and occasionally frustrating, and, above all, necessary if you want to reach your potential as a golfer.

◁ *The 'coach' is one of a number of products I use to help a student learn and appreciate the feel of a good swing.*

FIT FOR GOLF?: *Exercises for strength and flexibility*

ONE OF THE THINGS I have found in my teaching is that many players are physically incapable of achieving certain positions in the swing – most notably a complete backswing – for the simple reason that they don't have the necessary flexibility or suppleness to achieve a full turn.

I have always felt that being reasonably fit helps a player to build a good swing and maintain a consistent game. I'm not about to suggest that you run 10 miles a week and bench-press 300 lbs. But working on some basic exercises can help you increase your general strength and flexibility, which will benefit your swing and your stamina over 18 holes.

From an aerobic standpoint, walking is the most natural exercise of all, and regular walking – two or three miles three times a week – is hugely beneficial to your general level of fitness. Anything to get the heart-rate up and improve circulation. Jogging is not good for everyone, but a brisk walk keeps the legs strong and keeps you fit – mentally and physically. Not only will you feel better for it, you will remain focused and concentrate more thoroughly over the course of 18 holes.

I work out regularly, and am a big believer in the value of fitness – not simply for golf, but for enhancing the quality of life. If they don't already have one, I tell players who come to see me that they should develop some sort of exercise program. It helps to discipline your approach to getting better, and should become a natural part of your practice schedule. With the help of two experts in their respective fields – Chris Verna, a stretching and flexibility specialist, and Pat Etcheberry, strength and training consultant with the LGE Sports Science Group – here are some ideas that will help you to keep your body in shape and so allow you to play your best golf. They require little in the way of expensive equipment, and can be rehearsed easily at home.

IMPROVE FLEXIBILITY

THE SECRET TO DEVELOPING an upward cycle of flexibility is not determined by how much time you spend on the exercises shown here. It is the consistency of your exercise pattern that matters most, and that's why I encourage a 10-15 minute routine, to be repeated twice a day. I suggest stretching in the morning after a shower (you need to be alert, mentally, so don't do these exercises 'cold'), or as part of your warm-up routine before a game, and again in the evening, or after playing golf.

If you're having trouble making a swing change, or achieving a full turn, it may well be physical limitations that are holding you back. So work on these exercises and limber up your joints and muscles for the benefit of your game. This warm-up routine will help you to rebalance the muscles in your body, and set you on an upward cycle of improved flexibility.
Chris Verna

Squat for a better posture:
This squat motion will help to get the blood flowing to your thighs, and generally help you to adopt a sound athletic posture. Hold a club across your shoulders, and, from a regular posture, assume a sitting position; bend your knees and feel the tension build in the thighs as you lower and then raise your body.

The pivot motion:
Adopt a good posture, hold a club (or broom) across your shoulders, and simply work on the pivot motion. Try to achieve at least a 90° shoulder turn, both back and through. Go further if you can do so – push your limits. Hold the fully stretched backswing position for 15 seconds, relax, then do the same on the through-swing. As you do this, try to be aware of deep-breathing from your stomach. This will help to relax your whole body.

The quad stretch: Stretching the top of your quad muscles is important in terms of creating a sound posture and supporting a good turn of the upper body. To achieve this, stand and pull your foot up toward your butt as you bring your knees slightly back. Hold this position for 15 seconds. Do it twice, then repeat on the other side.

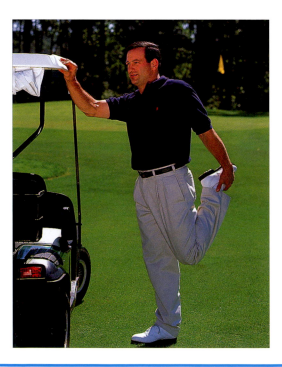

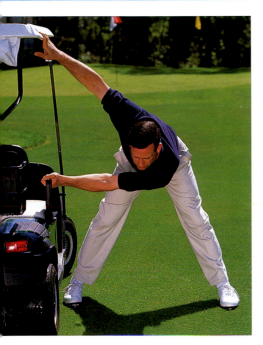

The shoulder stretch:
This is another exercise I recommend to stretch the shoulders, and you can do it either indoors or out on the course before a game. Again, create a good posture, then bend over until your shoulders are level with your hips, and grab a post (or some other firm object), as you see here. Keeping your shoulders perpendicular with your body, pull and push against the resistance. This is a great way to get rid of tension in the upper back, which helps you to make a fuller turn in the swing.

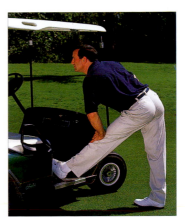

The hamstring stretch:
Stand and rest your foot on something secure (like a buggy). Straighten your leg, and hold that position for several seconds. As you do this, you will feel the hamstring at the back of the leg stretch. Hold this position for 15 seconds, then relax and repeat with the other leg.

Trunk flexibility:
Take hold of a club, stand up straight and arch your body first to the right, and then to the left. As you do so, hold the stretch position on each side for several seconds. Repeat five stretches per side.

Palm up, palm down:
Take a club, and with your hands about 12 inches apart, place the left hand palm down and the right hand palm up, as I am doing here. Then, from a good posture position, work on your trunk motion, going back and forth with a smooth rhythm. Keep your arms perfectly straight. That will help to stretch the middle part of your back, right along the spine.

EXERCISE FOR GREATER STRENGTH

OVER THE YEARS I have worked with many of the greatest names in golf – including Nick Faldo, Nick Price and Arnold Palmer. Players like this understand the importance of being in good physical condition in order to endure the time they spend hitting balls on the practice tee and the rigours of a 72-hole tournament, which are considerable. The common goal they share is wanting to increase strength, but not bulk.

Many of the back problems experienced in golf occur because of poor rotary motion, weak abdominal muscles and a lack of flexibility. If you cannot do physically what you hope to achieve technically, you are fighting a losing battle, but I would suggest that a comprehensive work-out can be achieved with these exercises in just 10 or 15 minutes.

First, a word of warning. If you have not taken regular exercise, start slowly and build repetition gradually. I believe repeating these exercises two or three times a week is ample – do that and you will see a dramatic improvement in your physical conditioning.
Pat Etcheberry

Abdominal crunches: This is one of the best exercises you can do to improve abdominal strength. Start by lying flat on your back, with your hands behind your head, and then raise your head as far as possible. You will feel the muscles contract immediately. Relax and repeat. Start with 10 repetitions, and rest for a minute between sets.

The step-up: Using a chair or a bench as a prop, repeat a simple step-up, step-down routine, leading first with the right foot for a series of 10 repetitions, and then the left. Repeat 1-3 sets, as you feel comfortable.

The lunge: From a standing start, with hands on hips, take a long step and hold the position for several seconds. You will feel this stretch in the back calf muscles and hamstring, which will build the strength in your legs and thighs needed for good golf. Relax and repeat.

Superman: Lie flat on your stomach with your hands behind your back and your feet together. Then do a 'Superman' – raise your legs, head and chest as if you were flying. Repeat in sets of 10 flights.

Wrist curl: If you don't have specialist weights at home, get yourself a plastic container and fill it with water (to whatever weight you feel comfortable with). Exercise your wrists and forearms with this basic wrist curl. Sit with your forearms resting on your thighs, and curl your wrists up and down as I am doing here. Repeat these curls in sets of 20.

The trunk drill: Hold the container with both hands at shoulder-height, and work on the rotary motion of your torso, swinging the container back and forth with a sweeping, circular motion. Repeat 1-3 sets of 15 repetitions.

Shoulder stretch: Now you are ready to work on the shoulder muscles with this basic fly-exercise. From a sitting position, bend forwards and raise the weights to shoulder-height. Do it slowly, and feel the muscles stretching under the pressure. Repeat 1-3 sets of 15. As you raise the container, imagine that you are pouring the water into glasses – that way you really give your arms and shoulders a full work-out.

EUROPE

CHART HILLS GOLF CLUB - EUROPEAN HEADQUARTERS
Contact: David Whelan
Weeks Lane, Biddenden, Kent, TN27 8JX, England
Phone: +(44) 1580 292117
CHGC Phone: +(44) 1580 292222
Fax: +(44) 1580 292118
CHGC Fax: +(44) 1580 292233

BAD TATZMANNSDORF
Contact: Kevyn Cunningham
Am Golfplatz 2, A-7431 Bad Tatzmannsdorf,
Austria
Phone: +(43) 3353 8282 780
Fax: +(43) 3353 8282 788
Hotel Fax: +(43) 3353 8841 55

GOLFY CLUB FRANCE
Contact: Jean Beauvillain
Golf de Montpellier-Massane, BP83,
34670 Baillargues, France
Phone: +(33) 4 67 91 25 37
Fax: +(33) 4 67 91 25 30

SPORTING CLUB BERLIN
Contact: Malcolm Joseph
Scharmutzelsee E.V., Parkallee 3,
D-15526 Bad Saarow, Germany
Phone: +(49) 33631 63300
Fax: +(49) 33631 63310

GOLF CLUB GUT WALDSHAGEN
Contact: Paul Dyer
24306 Gut Waldshagen, Germany
Phone: +(49) 45227 66777
Fax: +(49) 45227 66778

MT. JULIET
Contact: Mark Reid
Thomastown, County Kilkenny, Ireland
Phone: +(353) 56 24455
Fax: +(353) 56 24022

CARVOEIRO GOLFE S.A.
Contact: Sean Hogan
Apartado 11, Praia do Carvoeiro,
8401 Lagoa Codez, Algarve, Portugal
Phone: +(351) 82 34 2999
Fax: +(351) 82 34 2997

LA CALA RESORT
Contact: Paul Aitken
La Cala de Mijas, 29649 Mijas-Costa, Malaga, Spain
Phone: +(34) 5 266 9037
Fax: +(34) 5 266 9038

UNITED STATES

DAVID LEADBETTER GOLF ACADEMY -
CORPORATE HEADQUARTERS
Contact: Terri Leitner-Rice, Gary Gilchrist
1414 69th Avenue West, Bradenton, FL 34207
Phone: +(1) 941 739 2483
Fax: +(1) 941 751 0164

LAKE NONA GOLF CLUB
Contact: Patti McGowan
9100 Chiltern Drive, Orlando, FL 32827
Phone: +(1) 407 857 8276
Fax: +(1) 407 857 6590

QUAIL WEST GOLF AND COUNTRY CLUB
Contact: Adam Bazalgette
6303 Burnham Road, Naples, FL 34119
Phone: +(1) 941 592 1444
Fax: +(1) 941 592 1040

DESERT WILLOW GOLF RESORT
Contact: Adam Schriber
Palm Desert, CA 92253
Phone: +(1) 619 564 0777

HAMLET WINDWATCH (Seasonal)
Contact: Jeff Saager
1715 Vanderbilt Motor Pkwy, Hauppage, NY 11788
Phone +(1) 212 772 8900
Fax: +(1) 212 772 2617

CARMEL VALLEY RANCH (Seasonal)
Contact: Adam Schriber
One Old Ranch Road, Carmel, CA 93923
Phone: +(1) 408 626 2510
Fax: +(1) 408 626 2532

ASIA

DLGA, PRESS COUNTRY CLUB
Contact: Kevin Smeltz
4816 Banchi 1, Shimoakima, Annaka-shi
Gunma Prefecture, Japan 379-01
Phone: + (81) 2 7381 3727
Fax: +(81) 2 7382 2277

THANA CITY GOLF AND COUNTRY CLUB, LTD.
Contact: Steve Wakulsky
100-100/1 Moo 4, KM 14, Bangna Trad Highway,
Bangchalong, Bangplee, Samutprakarn 10540
Bangkok, Thailand
Phone: +(66) 23 361 9719
Fax: +(66) 23 361 980